THE PILLOW-BOOK OF
SEI SHŌNAGON

TRANSLATED BY

ARTHUR WALEY

GROVE PRESS, INC. NEW YORK

TO
HAZEL CROMPTON

First Evergreen Edition 1960

MANUFACTURED IN THE UNITED STATES OF AMERICA

PRELIMINARY NOTES

1. I have here translated about a quarter of the *Pillow-Book*.[1] Omissions have been made only where the original was dull, unintelligible, repetitive, or so packed with allusion that it required an impracticable amount of commentary.

2. Short extracts from the *Pillow-Book* will be found in Aston's *Japanese Literature* (1899), Florenz's *Geschichte der Jap. Litteratur* (1906), and Revon's *Anthologie de la Littérature Japonaise* (1910). Save for a line or two here and there, and two anecdotes (pp. 78 and 113), parts of which are translated by Aston and Revon, I have avoided what has been translated before, not on principle, but because it seemed to me that, on the whole, the least interesting passages had been chosen.[2]

[1] *Makura no Sōshi*, this being a name given at the time to notebooks in which stray impressions were recorded.

[2] Since this was written there has appeared *Les Notes de l'Oreiller*, by K. Matsuo and Steinilber-Oberlin, containing

3. The text I have used is that of the *Makura no Sōshi Hyōshaku* (first published, 1924; 2nd edition in one volume, 1926), by Kaneko Moto-omi, to whose commentary I am greatly indebted. The proofs have been read by Miss Sybil Pye and Mr. Tadao Doi, to both of whom I am very grateful.

extracts which amount, like mine, to about a quarter of the original. My selection was, however, made from a very different point of view and coincides with theirs only to the extent of a few pages. The two books are therefore complementary.

THE PILLOW-BOOK OF SEI SHŌNAGON

JAPAN IN THE TENTH CENTURY

WHEN the first volume of *The Tale of Genji* appeared in English, the prevailing comment of critics was that the book revealed a subtle and highly developed civilization, the very existence of which had hitherto remained unsuspected. It was guessed that so curious a state of society, with its rampant æstheticism and sophisticated unmorality, its dread of the explicit, the emphatic, must have behind it a protracted history of undisturbed development, or (as others put it) must be the climax of an age-long decadence.

And it is indeed true that the unique civilization portrayed in the *Tale of Genji* and *The Pillow-Book* of Sei Shōnagon corresponds to a unique record of isolation and tranquillity. The position of Japan, lying on the edge of the

Oriental world, has been compared to that of England always in full communion with Europe, yet exempt from the worst perils of contiguity —in fact, ideally 'semi-detached.'

But the comparison has little force. Japan is eight times farther from the mainland than we from France. One cannot swim across the Straits of Tsushima. Yet phase after phase of civilization—agriculture, tools, domestic animals at an age long before history, then later, the Chinese ideograms, Indian religion, Persian textiles—managed to filter across the Straits; while invasion, save for an occasional raid of pirates from China, not merely during those early years, but until the abortive Mongol descent in the thirteenth century, was almost unknown. In Europe and on the continent of Asia no single strip of land has ever enjoyed a like immunity. Across France, Hungary, Poland, Turkestan, how many armies marched during the long centuries of Japan's absolute security! Thus arose a culture that, among other peculiarities, had that of not being cosmopolitan. Rome, Byzantium, Ctesiphon, even Ch'ang-an were international cities. In the streets of Kyōto a stray Korean or Chinaman were, as specimens of the exotic, the best that could be hoped for. The world, to a Japanese of the tenth century, meant Japan and China. India was semi-mythical, and Persia uncertainly poised somewhere between China and Japan.

Thus, since the establishment of the capital at Heian [1] in 794, had grown up a highly specialized, intense and uniform civilization, dominated by one family, the Fujiwara; a state of society in which the stock of knowledge, the experience, the prejudices of all individuals were so similar that the grosser forms of communication seemed no longer necessary. A phrase, a clouded hint, an allusion half-expressed, a gesture imperceptible to common eyes, moved this courtly herd with a facility as magic as those silent messages that in the prairie ripple from beast to beast.

It was a purely æsthetic and, above all, a literary civilization. Never, among people of exquisite cultivation and lively intelligence, have purely intellectual pursuits played so

[1] Often referred to as Kyōto, i.e. the Capital.

small a part. What strikes us most is that the past was almost a blank; not least so the history of Japan, extending even in mythological theory only to the seventh century B.C. and remaining fabulous for fifteen hundred years.

It is indeed our intense curiosity about the past that most sharply distinguishes us from the ancient Japanese. Here every educated person is interested in some form or another of history. The busiest merchant is an authority upon snuff-boxes, Tudor London, or Chinese jade. The remotest country clergyman reads papers on eoliths; his daughters revive forgotten folk-dances. But to the Japanese of the tenth century, 'old' meant fusty, uncouth, disagreeable. To be 'worth looking at' a thing must be *imamekashi*, 'now-ish,' up-to-date. By Shōnagon and Murasaki the great collection of early poetry (the *Manyōshū*), on the rare occasions when they quote it, is always referred to in an apologetic way, as something which despite its solid merits will necessarily offend the modern eye. Nor did they feel that the future—with us an increasing preoccupation—in any way concerned them.

Their absorption in the present, the fact that
with them 'modern' was invariably a term of
praise, differentiates them from us in a way that
is immediately obvious. The other aspects of
their intellectual passivity—the absence of
mathematics, science, philosophy (even such
amateur speculation as amused the Romans was
entirely unknown)—may not seem at first sight
to constitute an important difference. Scientists
and philosophers, it is true, exist in modern
Europe. But to most of us their pronounce-
ments are as unintelligible as the incantations of
a Lama; we are mere drones, slumbering amid
the clatter of thoughts and contrivances that
we do not understand and could still less ever
have created. If the existence of contemporary
research had no influence except upon those
capable of understanding it, we should indeed
be in much the same position as the people
of Heian. But, strangely enough, something
straggles through; ideas which we do not completely understand modify our perceptions and
hence refashion our thoughts to such an extent
that the society lady who said 'Einstein means
so much to me' was expressing a profound truth.

It is, then, not only their complete absorption in the passing moment, but more generally the entire absence of intellectual background that makes the ancient Japanese so different from us, and gives even to the purely æsthetic sides of their culture a curious quality of patchiness. At any moment these men and women, to all appearances so infinitely urbane and sophisticated, may surprise us, even where matters of taste rather than intellect are concerned, by lapsing into a *niaiserie* far surpassing the silliness of our own Middle Ages. It is this insecurity which gives to the Heian period that oddly evasive and, as it were, two-dimensional quality, its figures and appurtenances seeming to us sometimes all to be cut out of thin, transparent paper.

Religious ceremonies were much in vogue, but were viewed chiefly from an æsthetic standpoint. The recitation of sacred texts was an art practised by the laity as well as the clergy. An exacting standard of connoisseurship prevailed, and if Buddhist services were packed to overflowing, it was upon appraising the merits of the performers rather than upon his own spiritual improvement that a Heian worshipper was bent.

Mimes, pageants, processions filled the Court calendar. Those organized by the Church had a certain tinge of exotic solemnity; for till the tenth century Indian Buddhism continued to send out fresh waves of influence, which now reached China (and hence Japan) less circuitously than in former days.

But it would scarcely be an exaggeration to say that the real religion of Heian was the cult of calligraphy. Certainly writing was the form of conduct that was scrutinized most severely. We find beauty of penmanship not merely counting for almost as much as beauty of person, but spoken of rather as a virtue than as a talent, and the epithet 'good,' when applied to an individual, frequently refers not to conduct but to handwriting. Often in Japanese romances it is with some chance view of the heroine's writing that a love-affair begins; and if the hero happens to fall in love with a lady before he has seen her script, he awaits the first 'traces of her hand' with the same anxiety as that which afflicted a Victorian gentleman before he had ascertained his fiancée's religious views. It was as indispensable that a Japanese mistress should write beautifully as that Mrs. Gladstone should be sound about the episcopal succession.

Again, a considerable place in the lives of the ancient Japanese was given to arts the very existence of which the West has barely recognized. For example, the art of blending perfumes, regarded by us as a mere trade, ranked in ancient Japan as the equal of music and poetry.

These things, however, are only differences of emphasis. Calligraphy has perhaps nowhere else so nearly achieved the status of a religion; but it has been practised as an art throughout the East, and was esteemed at certain moments even in Europe. So recently as the beginning of the present century a small school, led by Dr. Bridges, gave it a considerable prominence in one part of England. And even the burning of perfumes, though on the whole neglected in this country, has always been practised here and there, experimentally, in corners that some chance has screened from the censure of Nordic virility.

Again, the purely æsthetic approach to

religion, which was the rule in Heian, has often been fostered in Europe by cliques of exceptional people. At first sight, indeed, Buddhism (with its rosaries, baptism, tonsured monks, and nuns; its Heaven, Purgatory, and Hell) appears to have many points of resemblance to Catholic Christianity. But I fancy, all the same, that the most fundamental difference between the Japanese (or, for that matter, any Far Eastern nation) and us is the fact, obvious indeed yet constantly overlooked, that they were not Christians.

The Buddhist is taught that the world of appearances, with all its imperfection, is coeval with Buddha (using the name in its metaphysical not its historical sense). He is, in fact, this world, and does not exist outside it. Impossible, then, to reproach him with its sorrow or iniquity. The Christian (or strictly, the adherent of any Semitic religion; for it holds good of the Moslem and Jew) alone has compassed the magnificent conception of a Being all-wise, all-powerful, the incarnation of Good. But the world (His creation) is patently evil. Is there then some mistake? Is this adored Being in reality powerless against evil, or ignorant, or cruel? These are the questions that in all ages have racked the Christian's soul. Official solutions (which it was heresy to reject) failed to satisfy him; the conflict became an agony that has continually goaded Western man into what to the East have seemed gratuitous turmoils and achievements, making his thoughts a hard bed to lie on, waking him (as uneasy quarters drive a traveller on to the road at dawn) not only to fresh adventures but to the discovery of beauties that, wrapped in morning dreams, the East has ignored.

It has been suggested, as a dominating characteristic of the ancient Japanese, that they were without a sense of sin. It would, I maintain, be truer to say that they were not troubled by the Problem of Evil. But a sense of sin they certainly did not lack. Hell gaped at them perpetually; no delicately Japanicized variety, but a true Dantesque inferno, brutally depicted not only on monastery walls, but even amid the gay elegancies of the Palace. The period at which Shōnagon wrote her book corresponded with a time of general panic concerning the Life to Come. In 985 appeared Eshin Sōzu's *Ōiō*

Yōshū or 'Texts Essential to Salvation,' with its ghoulish evangelism that culminated in the great democratic 'revivals' of Hōnen Shōnin in the twelfth and Shinran in the thirteenth century.

And if Eshin's mission marked the beginning of a new phase in Japanese religion, it was at the same time associated with the political counter-currents that ultimately destroyed the civilization of Heian.

Among Eshin's aristocratic adherents the most important were drawn not from the dominant Fujiwara family but its rivals, the Taira and Minamoto.[1] One of his most influential followers was Taira no Koremochi, a lawless character, possibly the model for Murasaki's Tayū (the braggadocio suitor of Tamakatsura) in the third volume of *Genji*. Koremochi had a dispute with one of the Fujiwaras about a piece of land, and failing to win his case, waylaid and slaughtered his rival. The consequences of this murder, committed with

[1] E.g. Taira no Koremochi and Minamoto no Mitsunaka. But the point should not be pressed; for Eshin was also patronized by the Emperor's mother, who was a Fujiwara.

complete impunity, were far-reaching. For centuries the Fujiwaras had been hedged round by
a mysterious prestige. Fiefs, titles, offices of
state—all seemed to belong to them by some
inviolable decree, and each fresh claim met only
with a superstitious acquiescence. But now it
had been discovered, to everyone's astonishment, that even a Fujiwara could crumple at
the touch of steel, 'roll over like an ox and
vanish unavenged.' These events took place in
the extreme north of the main Island. Here,
and in all the border provinces the hold of the
Fujiwaras was beginning to weaken. The great
struggle began early in the twelfth century; but
when it came it was a contest not between
civilization and barbarism—for the effeminate
and decadent society of Heian disappeared at
the first breath of conflict—but between a long
series of rival swashbucklers and dictators. And
with the advent of a robust militarism the old
attitude towards religion, half childish, half
cynical, gave way on the one hand to the
intense, peasant faith of Hōnen, and on the
other to the passionate mysticism of the Nō plays.

The life of the Heian Court in the tenth

century is known to us chiefly through two documents, *The Tale of Genji*, a novel by Murasaki Shikibu, and *The Pillow-Book* by Sei Shōnagon. The first has, as a document, the disadvantage of being fiction. Murasaki shows us the world, particularly the male part of it, rather as she would like it to have been than as she actually found it. She dreamed of lovers who, though in every sense men, should yet retain the gentleness and grace of her girl friend Saishō.[1] How different was the world she actually lived in we can see in her *Diary*, which fortunately is also preserved.

The *Pillow-Book*, on the other hand, is a plain record of fact, and being at least ten times as long as Murasaki's *Diary*, and far more varied in contents, it is the most important document of the period that we possess.[2]

[1] See *A Wreath of Cloud* (*Genji*, part iii), p. 22.

[2] In *Court Ladies of Old Japan* (Constable, 1921) two diaries of the period, as well as that of Murasaki, are translated. Of these, the 'Diary of Izumi Shikibu' is not a genuine document, but a romance written round the well-known story of Izumi's love-affairs; the *Sarashina Diary* is a much worked-up and highly literary production. For the *Kagerō nikki*, 'Gossamer Diary,' see introduction to *The Tale of Genji*, vol. ii.

Sei Shōnagon, the authoress of the *Pillow-Book*, was born in 966 or 967, the daughter of Kiyohara no Motosuke. The Kiyohara clan was descended from Temmu, the fortieth Emperor of Japan. For many generations, Motosuke's ancestors had held office as provincial governors, a respectable but undistinguished form of employment. Chiefly, however, they are known for their devotion to learning and literature. Prince Toneri, the founder of the family, was one of the compilers of the *Nihongi*, or 'Chronicles of Japan';[1] another ancestor, Natsuno,[2] who died in 837, was the author of an important work, the *Ryō no gige* or 'Commentary on the Penal Code,' while Shōnagon's great-grandfather, Fukayabu, became the typical Court-poet of the early tenth century, and his thin elegant verse still figures in every anthology.

Motosuke held a series of governorships; but he, too, is best known as a poet and student of poetry. He lectured upon the text of the *Man-*

---

[1] Finished in A.D. 720. Translated by W. G. Aston.

[2] He also organized the building of the great harbour at Uozumi.

yōshū, a collection of ancient poems that were already becoming difficult to understand, and was one of the compilers of the *Gosenshū*, the second official anthology. He was appointed to his last governorship, that of Bingo, in 986 and died in 990.

A year later Shōnagon, now aged about twenty-four, entered the service of the little Empress Sadako, who had arrived at Court the year before. The Empress, a daughter of the Prime Minister, Fujiwara no Michitaka, was now fifteen: she died in childbirth ten years later, and it is with these years, from 991 to 1000, that the *Pillow-Book* deals.

It consists partly of reminiscences, partly of entries in diary-form. The book is arranged not chronologically, but under a series of headings, such as 'Disagreeable Things,' 'Amusing Things,' 'Disappointing Things,' and the like; but often this scheme breaks down and the sequence becomes entirely arbitrary.

To keep some kind of journal was a common practice of the day. No other miscellany like the *Pillow-Book* exists; but there may well have been others, for Heian literature has not survived in its entirety. Thus, Shōnagon gives us a list of her favourite novels. Out of eleven, only one (*The Hollow Tree*) survives; and from other sources we know the names of over twenty novels belonging to this period, all of which are lost. The question whether the particular form in which she cast her book, that of grouping the entries under headings such as 'disagreeable things,' 'amusing things,' etc., was suggested to her by some previous work is difficult to decide. There exists a book [1] by the Chinese poet Li Shang-yin (813–58) called *Tsa Tsuan*, or 'Miscellaneous Notes,' which is arranged on this principle, though its matter is very different, the author remaining content with mere enumerations, for example:

Things that certainly won't come.

A dog, if called to by a man with a stick in his hand.

A singing-girl, if summoned by a penniless student.

---

[1] Only 26 pages long. It is contained in the *T'ang Tai Ts'ung Shu*, or Minor Works of the T'ang dynasty.

Inappropriate Things.

For a Persian to be poor. For a doctor to fall ill. For a schoolmaster not to recognize an ideogram. For a butcher to recite the Scriptures.[1]

Things that make a Bad Impression.

To fall off one's horse at polo. To choke when eating with one's superiors. To return to worldly life after having been in a monastery or convent. To lie on someone else's bed with one's boots on. To sing love-songs in the presence of one's parents.

Whereas Shōnagon almost always illustrates her categories by long anecdotes and reminiscences, the Chinese writer, as we have seen, confines himself to bald lists. Shōnagon is concerned with her own likes and irritabilities; Li Shang-yin merely expresses a sort of generalized proverbial wisdom. Her experience is drawn exclusively from the Court; his illustrations are drawn from market-place and farm.

Despite these differences, the particular form in which the *Pillow-Book* is cast might quite

---

[1] Buddhists being forbidden to kill.

conceivably be due to the *Tsa Tsuan*. The difficulty is that Li Shang-yin's book does not seem to have reached Japan till many centuries later. That no single copy of the *Tsa Tsuan* existed in Japan at a particular date is a thing that obviously cannot be proved. The question is not in itself of much importance, but it is worth mentioning in order to call attention to the Chinese book, which is a singularly interesting document of social history.

Shōnagon protests, as do most diarists and makers of journals, that the *Pillow-Book* was intended for herself alone. But it quickly fell into other hands. In 1002 she writes:

When the present Captain of the Bodyguard of the Left (Minamoto no Tsunefusa) was governor of Ise (i.e. in 995 or 996) he one day called on me at my home. By accident a mattress that was pushed out into the front room for him to sit on had my book lying on it. The moment I realized this I snatched at the book and made frantic efforts to recover it. But Tsunefusa carried it off with him and did not return it till a long time afterwards.

So far as I remember, this was the beginning of my book being handed about at Court.

What Tsunefusa saw and handed round in 995–6 was, of course, only part of the work, most of it having been written later than this.

Printing did not become general in Japan till the seventeenth century. The *editio princeps* of the *Pillow-Book* is in movable type and is said to date from the Keichō Period, 1596–1614. Many mediæval manuscript-copies exist; but their relative age and trustworthiness have not been fully investigated.

Concerning her arrival at Court, Shōnagon writes as follows:

When I first entered her Majesty's service I felt indescribably shy, and was indeed constantly on the verge of tears. When I came on duty the first evening, the Empress was sitting with only a three-foot screen in front of her, and so nervous was I that when she passed me some picture or book to look at, I was hardly capable of putting out my hand to take it. While she was talking about what she wanted me to see—telling me what it was or who had made it—I was all the time wondering whether my hair was in order. For the lamp was not in the middle of the room, but on a stand immediately beside where we sat, and we were more exposed than we should have been even by daylight. It was all I could do to fix my attention on what I was looking at. Only part of her Majesty's hand showed, for the weather was very cold and she had muffled herself in her sleeves; but I could see that it was pink and very lovely. I gazed and gazed. To an inexperienced home-bred girl like me it was a wonderful surprise to discover that such people as this existed on earth at all. At dawn I hurried away, but the Empress called after me, saying I seemed to be as frightened of the daylight as the ugly old God of Katsuragi.[1] I lay down again, purposely choosing an attitude in which she could not get a full view of me. The shutters had not yet been opened. But soon one of the ladies came along and the Empress called out to her, 'Please open those things!' She was beginning to do so, when the Empress suddenly said, 'Not now!'

[1] Who is so unhappy about his appearance that he hides all day and only comes out at night.

and, laughing, the lackey withdrew. Her Majesty then engaged me in conversation for some time, and said at last: 'Well, I expect you are wanting to be off. Go as soon as you like.' 'And come back in good time to-night,' she added. It was so late when I got back to my room that I found it all tidied and opened up for the day. The snow outside was lovely. Presently there came a message from the Empress saying it was a good opportunity for me to wait upon her in the morning. 'The snow-clouds make it so dark,' she said, 'that you will be almost invisible.' I could not bring myself to go, and the message was repeated several times. At last the head-girl of our room said: 'You mustn't shut yourself up here all the time. You ought to be thankful to get a chance like this. Her Majesty would not ask for you unless she really wanted you, and she will think it very bad manners if you do not go.' So I was hustled off, and arrived once more in the Imperial Presence, in a state of miserable embarrassment and confusion.

Shōnagon goes on to describe the ease and

nonchalance with which those in attendance upon the Empress went about their duties or lay 'with their Chinese cloaks trailing across the floor.' 'How I envied the composure with which they took and handed on the Empress's notes and letters, standing up and sitting down, talking and laughing without the slightest trace of embarrassment! Would a time ever come when I should feel equally at home in such surroundings? The mere thought made me tremble. ... Presently there were loud cries of "Make way!" Someone said it was the Prime Minister, and a great scuffling began, everyone clutching at whatever possessions they had left lying about and making hastily for the alcove.'

Shōnagon goes on to tell us that the visitor turns out to be not Michitaka, the Prime Minister, but his son, Korechika, the Empress's favourite brother, then a lad of eighteen.

KORECHIKA. These last two days I have been supposed to be in retreat.[1] But I wanted to see how you were getting on in this tremendous snow-storm.

[1] For Buddhist observances.

EMPRESS. I did not expect you. I thought 'no roads were left. . . .'[1]

KORECHIKA. Did you think that would stop me? I made sure 'your heart was filled with pity. . . .'

What, I thought, could have been more elegant than such a conversation as this? It was up to the most high-flown passages in any of the novels I had read. . . . After a while my Lord Korechika asked who was behind the curtains-of-state, and someone having told him it was I, he rose to his feet, intending, as I first thought, to go away. But instead, he came close up to the curtains and spoke about something that he heard had happened to me before I came to Court. I had already been feeling utterly awe-struck as I gazed at him through the curtains; and now when he actually came up and began to address me, I almost fainted.

Sometimes at festivals and processions he

[1] In allusion to the poem: 'In this mountain village, after the snow-storm, no roads are left; and my heart is full of pity for him who I know will come.' Taira no Kanemori, the author of this poem, had died a few months before.

had seemed to be looking in the direction of our carriage; whereupon we had immediately made fast the blinds and even hidden our faces with our fans, lest he should get a momentary view of our profiles. And now, sitting terror-stricken before him, I wondered how it was that I had ever consented to embark upon a career for which I was so hopelessly ill-qualified. Even the fan with which I was attempting to hide my embarrassment he now took from me. I felt certain at once that my hair was straggling down in the wildest disorder, and whether it really was or no, probably I looked quite as distraught as I was feeling. Twisting my fan in his fingers, he began asking who painted it, and other questions—I all the while hoping only that he would soon go away. But it was clear he had no intention of doing so, for he was now reclining on his back close to the curtains.   I think her Majesty felt at last that his long stay was disconcerting me, for she called to him: 'Come over here! I want you to tell me whose writing this is.' How thankful I felt! But Lord Korechika replied: 'Send it along and I will look at it!' and when she still insisted that he should come to her, he said: 'I would come; but Shōnagon here has hold of me and will not let go.' This, of course, was whimsical enough, but rather embarrassing for me, considering the immense difference in our ages and positions.

Her Majesty was now looking at some piece or other of writing in cursive syllabary. 'If you want to know who wrote it, show it to this lady. I'll be bound there's not a hand in the world that she would not recognize.' So he went on, always trying to say something that would get an answer out of me.

'Shōnagon, do you like me?' the Empress asked presently. 'Why, Madam, what else do you suppose?' I was beginning to reply, when someone in the breakfast-room sneezed violently. 'There!' cried her Majesty. 'That shows you are not telling the truth. Of course, it would be nice if you liked me, but it can't be helped.'

Next morning, when Shōnagon is in her room, someone brings her a note written on light green paper, and very prettily got up. In it is the poem: 'Never had I known, never had known that false was false; save for the God of Truth whose voice resounded in the empty air.' 'It had been dictated,' Shōnagon continues, 'to one of her ladies. I felt terribly mortified and confused. How I should have liked to get hold of the person who produced that unlucky sneeze!'

Shōnagon's reply—'Thankless my lot who, for the trespass of another's nose, am thought of shallow heart'—contains puns and ingenuities which it would be tedious to explain.

Thus began Shōnagon's career at Court. There are, however, in the *Pillow-Book* two passages which refèr to an earlier period in her life. In 986, when she was about twenty, she attended a Buddhist Ceremony at the palace of Fujiwara no Naritoki, Colonel of the Body-guard and Assistant Councillor of State. 'The heat,' she says, 'was desolating, and we had things to attend to that could not be left over till next day; so we meant only to hear a little of the service and then go home. But such surging oceans of carriages had pressed in behind us, that it was impossible to escape.

When the morning part of the ceremony was over we sent word to the carriages at the back of us that we were going away, and being glad enough to get a little closer, they at once let us through, and themselves moved up into line. We had to put up with a good deal of chaffing as we retired. . . . His lordship Yoshichika [1] called to me as we passed: "You *do well to retire*." At the moment I was suffering so much from the heat that I did not see the point: but afterwards I sent a man to him with the message: "Among five thousand arrogants, you too will surely find a place." '

The allusion (and nothing would so have covered Shōnagon with shame as that it should be thought she had not recognized it) is to a passage in the *Lotus Sūtra* where five thousand of Buddha's hearers walk out during one of his sermons. Buddha makes no attempt to stop them, saying only: 'Arrogant creatures, *they do well to retire*.' It is precisely this part of the *Lotus Sūtra* that is read at the end of the morning service on the first day of the ceremony in question, so that Shōnagon, who became the

[1] Another Fujiwara grandee, a distant cousin of their host.

great pastmaster in the art of capping quotations, begins her career with a very light ordeal.

The following passage also seems to belong to about the year 986:

On that day too (the seventh of the first month) I loved being taken to see the White Horses.[1] We girls living at home used to drive off to the Palace in a coach marvellously furbished. When we came to the ground-bar of the Middle Gate, there was always a terrible bump. Heads knocked together, combs fell out, and, if one did not instantly rescue them, got trampled upon and smashed to pieces. Near the guard-room were a lot of officers, who used to take bows from soldiers in the procession and twang them, to make the White Horses prance. This we found very entertaining. In the distance, through one of the gates of the Inner Palace, we could see shutters, behind which figures were moving to and fro, ladies perhaps of the Lamp or Wardrobe. How marvellous they seemed to us—these people who walked about the Palace as though it belonged to them!

[1] Twenty-one of them were led in procession.

So close did the procession pass that one could study the very texture of the soldiers' faces. I remember one who had put on his powder unevenly, so that here and there his dark skin showed through, looking like those black patches in the garden, when the snow has begun to melt. An absurd sight. But when the horses reared and plunged wildly about I was frightened, and shrinking back into our coach saw nothing more of the show.

Here is an after-breakfast scene in the Palace, dating from the spring of 994:

Presently we heard those who had been handing the Imperial Dishes tell the serving-men they might clear, and a moment later His Majesty reappeared. He asked me to mix some ink ... and presently folded a white poem-slip, saying to us gentlewomen: 'Write me a few scraps of old poetry—anything that comes into your head.' I asked my lord Kore-chika what he advised me to choose. 'Don't ask me,' he said. 'Write something quickly and hand it in. This is entirely your affair. We men are not intended to help you.' And he put the inkstand by me, adding: 'Don't stop to think! The *Naniwazu* [1] or anything else you happen to know. . . .' Really there was nothing to be afraid of; but for some reason I felt terribly confused, and the blood rushed to my face. Two or three of the upper ladies tried their hands, one with a spring song, another with a poem on this or that flower. Then it came to me, and I wrote out the poem: 'The years go by; age and its evils crowd upon me, but be this as it may, while flowers are here to see, I cannot grieve.' But instead of 'flowers' I wrote 'my Lord.' 'I did this out of curiosity,' said the Emperor, while he was looking at what I had written. 'It is so interesting to see what is going on in people's heads.' A conversation followed, in the course of which he said: 'I remember my father, the late Emperor Enyū, once [2] saying to his gentlemen-in-attendance: "Here is a book. Each of you shall write a poem in it." Several of them found great difficulty in getting started. "Don't bother about your handwriting,"

[1] The first poem that children learned to write.
[2] Probably in 984.

my father said, "nor, for that matter, whether your poems are suitable to the season. It's all one to me." Thus encouraged (but still making rather a burden of it) they set to work. One of them was the present Prime Minister! He was only a captain of the Third Rank then. When it came to his turn he wrote the old poem: "Like the tide that rises on the shore of Izumo, deeper and deeper grows my love for you; yes, mine." But he altered "love for you" to "devotion to my Sovereign," which pleased my father very much.'

Shōnagon then tells us of the Emperor's astonishment that people should be able to read such vast quantities of poetry. Twenty chapters (the length of the *Kokinshū*, the first official anthology) was far too much. 'I am sure for my part,' said the Emperor, 'I shall never succeed in getting beyond Chapter 2.'

Another extract:
From the beginning of the fifth month,¹ it had been dark, rainy weather all the time. I became so bored that at last I suggested we

¹ Of the year 995.

had better go out and see if we couldn't somewhere hear the cuckoo singing. This idea was
very well received, and one of the girls suggested we should try that bridge behind the
Kamo Shrine (it isn't called Magpie Bridge,
but something rather like it). She said that
there was a cuckoo there every day. Someone
else said it was not a cuckoo at all, but a cricket.
However, on the morning of the fifth day, off
we went. When we ordered the carriage, the
men said they didn't suppose that in such
weather as this anyone would mind if we were
picked up outside our own quarters and taken
out by the Northern Gate.[1] There was only
room for four. Some of the other ladies asked
whether we should mind their getting another
carriage and coming too. But the Empress
said 'No,' and though they were very much
disappointed we drove off rather hard-heartedly
without attempting to console them or indeed
worrying about them at all. Something seemed
to be happening at the riding-ground, where
there was a great press of people. When we

[1] Instead of walking to the Eastern Gate, the only one
which the Palace staff was supposed to use.

asked what was going on, we were told that the competitions were being held, and that the archers were just going to shoot on horseback. It was said, too, that the Officers of the Body-guard of the Left were there; but all we could see, when we had pulled up, was a few gentle-men of the Sixth Rank wandering vaguely about. 'Oh, do let us get on,' someone said; 'there's no one of any interest here.' So we drove on towards Kamo, the familiar road making us feel quite as though we were on our way to the Festival.[1] Presently we came to my lord Akinobu's[2] house, and someone suggested we should get out and have a look at it. Every-thing was very simple and countrified—pictures of horses on the panels, screens of wattled bam-boo, curtains of plaited grass—all in a style that seemed to be intentionally behind the times. The house itself was a poor affair and very cramped, but quite pretty in its way. As for cuckoos, we were nearly deafened! It is really a great pity her Majesty never hears

[1] The Kamo festival, in the fourth month.
[2] The Empress's maternal uncle. The Empress's mother came of a comparatively humble family.

them. And when we thought of the ladies who had wanted so badly to come with us, we felt quite guilty. 'It's always interesting to see things done on the spot,' said Akinobu, and sending for some stuff which I suppose was husked rice, he made some girls—very clean and respectable—along with others who seemed to come from neighbouring farms, show us how the rice was thrashed. Five or six of them did this, and then the grain was put into a sort of machine that went round, two girls turning it and at the same time singing so strange a song that we could not help laughing, and had soon forgotten all about the cuckoos. Then refreshments were brought on a queer old tray-stand such as one sees in Chinese pictures. As no one seemed much interested in its contents, our host said: 'This is rough, country fare. If you don't like it, the only thing to do in a place like this is to go on bothering your host or his servants till you get something you can eat. We don't expect you people from the Capital to be shy. These fern-shoots, now. I gathered them with my own hand.' 'You don't want us to arrange ourselves round the tray-stand like a lot of maid-servants sitting down to their supper?' I protested.

'Hand the things round,' he said . . . and while this was going on, in the midst of the clatter, one of the men came in and said that it was going to rain, and we hurried back to our carriage. I wanted to make my cuckoo-poem before we started; but the others said I could do it in the carriage. Before going we picked a huge branch of white-flower and decorated our carriage with it, great trails of blossom hanging over the windows and sides, till one would have thought a huge canopy of white brocade had been flung across the roof of the coach. Our grooms, throwing themselves into the thing, began with shouts of laughter squeezing fresh boughs of blossom into every cranny that would hold them. We longed to be seen by someone on our way back, but not a soul did we meet, save one or two wretched priests or other such uninteresting people. When we were nearly home we made up our minds it would be too dull to finish the day without anyone having seen us in our splendour, so we stopped at the palace in the First Ward and asked for the Captain,[1] saying we were just back from hearing the cuckoo. We were told he had been off-duty for some time and had got into easy clothes; but was now being helped into his Court trousers. Wouldn't we wait? We said we couldn't do that, and were driving on to the Eastern Gate, when he suddenly appeared running after us down the road. He had certainly changed in a marvellously short space of time, but was still buckling his belt as he ran. Behind him, barefooted in their haste, panted several dressers and grooms. We called to the coachman to drive on and had already reached the gate when, hopelessly out of breath, he staggered up to us. It was only then that he saw how we were decorated. 'This is a fairy chariot,' he laughed. 'I do not believe there are real people in it. If there are, let them get down and show themselves.'

'But, Shōnagon, what poems did you make to-day? That's what I should like to hear.' 'We're keeping them for her Majesty,' I replied. Just then it once more began to rain in

[1] Fujiwara no Kiminobu, aged eighteen; cousin of the Empress.

earnest. 'I have always wondered,' he said, 'why when all the other gates have arches, this Eastern gate should have none. To-day, for example, one badly needs it.' 'What am I to do now?' he asked presently. 'I was so determined to catch you up that I rushed out without thinking what was to become of me afterwards.' 'Don't be so ridiculous,' I said. 'You can come with us to the Palace.' 'In an *eboshi*?' [1] he asked. 'What can you be thinking of?' 'Send someone to fetch your hat,' I suggested. But it was now raining badly and our men, who had no rain-coats with them, were pulling in the carriage as quickly as they could.[2] One of his men presently arrived from his palace with an umbrella, and under its shelter he now, with a slow reluctance that contrasted oddly with his previous haste, made his way home, continually stopping to look back at us over his shoulder. With his umbrella in one hand and a bunch of white-flower in the other, he was an amusing sight.

When we were back in the Palace, her

[1] A soft, high-crowned cap.
[2] The bulls that drew it had to be unyoked at the Palace gate.

Majesty asked for an account of our adventures. The girls who had been left behind were at first inclined to be rather sulky; but when we described how the Captain had run after us down the Great Highway of the First Ward, they could not help laughing. Presently the Empress asked about our poems, and we were obliged to explain that we had not made any. 'That is very unfortunate,' she said. 'Some of the gentlemen at Court are bound to hear of your excursion, and they will certainly expect something to have come of it. I can quite understand that on the spot it was not very easy to write anything. When people make too solemn an affair of such things, one is apt suddenly to feel completely uninterested. But it is not too late. Write something now. You're good for that much, surely.' This was all true enough; but it turned out to be a painful business. We were still trying to produce something when a messenger arrived, with a note from the Captain. It was written on thin paper stamped with the white-flower pattern, and was attached to the spray that he had taken from our carriage. His poem said: 'Would that of this journey I had heard. So had my heart been with you when you sought the cuckoo's song.' Fearing that we were keeping the messenger waiting, her Majesty sent round her own writing-case to our room, with paper slipped into the lid. 'You write something, Saishō,' I said. But Saishō was determined that I should write, and while we argued about it the sky suddenly grew .dark, rain began to pour, and there were such deafening peals of thunder, that we forgot all about our poem, and frightened out of our wits ran wildly from place to place, closing shutters and doors. The storm lasted a long time, and when at last the thunder became less frequent, it was already dark. We were just saying we really must get on with our answer, when crowds of visitors began to arrive, all anxious to talk about the storm, and we were obliged to go out and look after them. One of the courtiers said that a poem only needs an answer when it is addressed to someone in particular, and we decided to do no more about it. I said to the Empress that poetry seemed to have a bad *karma* to-day, and added that the best thing we could do was to keep as quiet as possible about our excursion. 'I still don't see why some of you who went should not be able to produce a few poems,' she replied, pretending to be cross. 'It isn't that you can't; of that I am sure. You have made up your minds not to.' 'The time has passed,' I said. 'One must do those things when one is in the right mood.' 'Right mood? What nonsense!' she exclaimed indignantly. But all the same, she did not worry me any more about it.

Two days afterwards Saishō was talking about our excursion, and mentioned the fern-shoots that Akinobu had 'plucked with his own hand.' The Empress was amused that Saishō seemed to have retained a much clearer memory of the refreshments than of anything else that happened during the expedition, and picking up a stray piece of paper she wrote: 'The memory of a salad lingers in her head,' and bade me make a beginning for the poem. I wrote: 'More than the cuckoo's song that she went out to hear.' 'Well, Shōnagon,' she said, laughing, 'how you of all people can have the face to mention cuckoos, I cannot imagine.' I felt very crestfallen, but answered boldly: 'I don't see anything to be ashamed of. I have made up my mind only to make poems when I feel inclined to. If, whenever there is a question of poetry, you turn upon me and ask me to compose, I shall stay in your service no longer. When I am called upon like that, I can't even count the syllables, still less think whether I am writing a winter song in spring, or a spring song in autumn. . . . I know there have been a lot of poets in my family; and it would certainly be very nice if, after one of these occasions, people said: "Of course, hers was much the best; but that is not surprising, considering what her father was." As it is, not having the slightest degree of special talent in that direction, I object strongly to being perpetually thrust forward and made to behave as though I thought myself a genius. I feel I am disgracing my father's memory!' I said this quite seriously; but the Empress laughed. However, she said I might do as I pleased, and promised that for her part she would never call upon me again. I felt immensely relieved.

. . . . Late one night when Korechika came in and began giving out themes upon which the ladies were to write poems, everyone else was delighted and poems were turned out in bundles. I meanwhile went on talking to the Empress about other matters. Presently Korechika caught sight of me and asked why I did not join the others and make some poems. 'Come and take your theme,' he said. I told him that I had, for good reasons of my own, given up writing poetry. This he was very loath to believe. 'I am sure,' he said, 'my sister would not allow you to do so. It is the most absurd thing I ever heard of. Well! you may do as you like on other occasions; but I am not going to let you off to-night.' However, I took no notice. While the poems of the other ladies were being judged, a minute slip of paper was handed to me by the Empress. On it was the poem: 'Shall she, who of the famed Motosuke an offspring is deemed, alone be missing from to-night's great tournament of song?' . . . To this I replied: 'Were I another's child, who sooner had enrolled in this night's tournament of song?' And I told the Empress, that if I were anyone else, I should be only too pleased to present her with thousands of poems.

A few weeks before the cuckoo-expedition, the Empress's father, the Prime Minister Michitaka had died at the early age of forty-eight. In the normal course of affairs he would have been succeeded by his eldest son, Korechika; for already the Fujiwaras had established a kind of kingship in Japan, at the expense of the Mikado, who, though he had to be handled according to certain fixed rules, was a mere pawn in their game. But Michitaka's brother, Michinaga, still a young man and with far more gift for politics than his nephew Korechika, was determined to shift the succession to his own branch of the family. For this purpose it was necessary to get up some kind of popular agitation against Korechika, and if possible to discredit his sister, the Empress Sadako, and replace her by a child of Michinaga's own. Just as Genji,[1] in a rather similar situation, gave a handle to his enemies by his impudent escapade with Oborozuki, so the Empress's brother Korechika lost no time in providing the opposing faction with a magnificent lever for his overthrow.

[1] See *The Sacred Tree*, p. 89.

49

We are now in the fourth month of 995. To understand how Korechika gave the desired opportunity to his enemies it is necessary to go back some years. In 984 the Emperor Kwazan had ascended the Throne at the age of sixteen. Almost immediately Kane-iye, the then Prime Minister, decided that the new Emperor was inconveniently old. He wanted to make an Empress of his grand-daughter, Sadako, a child of about ten. She could enter the Palace in a couple of years, but it would be a long time before she could be formally established as Empress. Meanwhile the Emperor would have grown to years of unmanageable discretion. A plot was hatched to replace Kwazan by his younger cousin, the subsequent Emperor Ichijō.[1] The problem was how to induce Kwazan to retire. The opportunity came when in 986 one of the Emperor's Court ladies, a certain Fujiwara no Tsuneko,[2] died suddenly. Kwazan was much affected, and obviously in a state of mind upon which it would be easy to work. Kane-iye's son Michikane went to the

[1] Then a child of four. His mother was Kane-iye's daughter.
[2] Second daughter of Kane-iye's brother, Tamemitsu.

KANE-IYE
- MICHITAKA
  - KORECHIKA
  - The Empress SADAKO, born 976. (Sei Shōnagon's Empress)
- MICHIKANE
- MICHINAGA
  - The Empress AKIKO (Murasaki's Empress)

TAMEMITSU (brother of Kane-iye)
- NARINOBU
- TADANOBU (Shōnagon's lover)
- KIMINOBU ('The Captain')
- TSUNEKO (Kwazan's concubine; died young)
- The Third Sister (courted by KORECHIKA)
- The Fourth Sister (courted by KWAZAN)

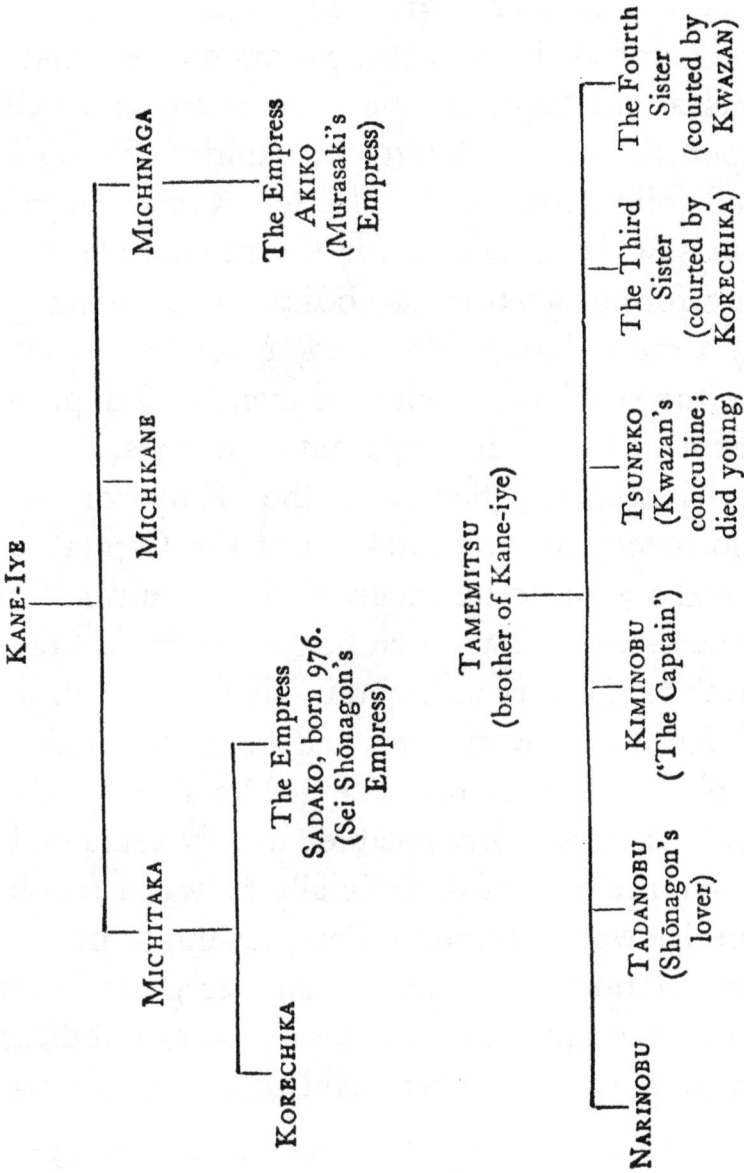

There was an elder sister (name unknown) who does not come into the story.

Palace and after a great harangue on the transience of all human things, announced that he was about to enter the priesthood, and called upon Kwazan to resign the vanities of kingship and follow him to the cloister. Kwazan agreed, but saw no necessity for the moment to make any formal gesture of abdication. Fearing that he would change his mind, Michikane packed up the regalia and with his own hand deposited them in the Heir Apparent's quarters.

Michikane then led the Emperor to a monastery on the outskirts of the Capital, and stood by while he received the tonsure. When it came to his own turn he said he must first go back to the City and obtain his father's consent.

Kwazan saw that he had been the victim of a plot and burst into tears. The step which he had taken was irrevocable; it only remained to make the best of it. Officially he was a monk in the Flower Mountain Temple; but it began to be rumoured that under another guise he was to be seen nightly in Kyōto. Kwazan abdicated in 986. In 995[1] it was said that he was secretly

[1] The year of the cuckoo-expedition that Shōnagon has just described.

frequenting the palace of the late High Falconer Tamemitsu—the very house from which 'the Captain' (Fujiwara no Kiminobu) had come running down the highway in pursuit of Shōnagon's carriage.

In the first month of 996, less than a year after his father's death, Korechika gave his enemies the opportunity for which they had been waiting.[1] He had for some while been in love with one of Kiminobu's sisters. He got it into his head that the ex-Emperor Kwazan was cutting him out. He stationed himself, along with his brother Taka-iye, outside Kiminobu's palace, and when a muffled figure crept out in the darkness, shot at it with his bow. Kwazan was wounded in the leg, but managed to crawl back to his monastery. The story leaked out, and both brothers were accused of sacrilege against the Church and the Imperial Family. It was no very reputable specimen either of royalty or priesthood who had been thus assaulted; but popular feeling, as regards the sanctity both of the Throne and the Church, was at that time passionate, and amid universal

[1] See above, p. 49.

reprobation Korechika was banished to Kyūshū, his brother to Izumo. The Empress Sadako seems to have shared to some extent in her brothers' disgrace. In the third month of 996 she left the Court and moved into her own house, the 'Small Palace in the Second Ward.' There was, however, an adequate reason for this removal. She was going to have a baby, and pregnant women were not allowed to remain in the Palace.

Only when all these commotions were over did Korechika discover that Kwazan's visits to the First Ward had been paid not, as rumour (which commonly makes light of such details) had informed him, to the Third Sister but to the Fourth, a lady in whom Korechika took no interest whatever.

The banishment of the young lords and the retirement from the Palace of the Empress Sadako were events which would in any case have moved Sei Shōnagon very deeply. It so happened, however, that she herself became unexpectedly involved. She had for years past carried on a desultory love-affair with Kiminobu's brother, Tadanobu. He was naturally furious at the scandal of his sister's connexion with the ex-Emperor becoming known, and openly sided with Korechika's prosecutors. It is likely enough that on some occasion, at a time when everyone's nerves were on edge, Shōnagon flared up on behalf of her lover.

In any case, she was regarded as being 'on the other side,' and after the Empress's move to the Second Ward, was allowed to remain in miserable suspense at her brother's house.

This went on for about four months. But in the autumn of 996 a certain captain of the Bodyguard of the Left told Shōnagon that he had been talking with some of the Empress's women, and had gathered from their conversation that her Majesty would welcome Shōnagon's return. 'At any rate go and have a look,' said the captain. 'The peonies in front of the terrace give the place an amusingly Chinese air. I am sure you would be delighted by it.' 'No,' she said, 'I don't like people thinking such things of me as they have thought.'

Shōnagon, however, relented, and soon afterwards we find her in the Small Palace. As I came from my room, she writes, I passed a group of ladies who were whispering together. I caught something about 'being in with Michinaga's party'; but when they saw me coming, they stopped talking, and edged away from me in so hostile a manner that I made up my mind I would not enter the Presence. This went on for several weeks, and though I was constantly asked to return, I would not do so; for I was sure that those about the Empress were all the while telling her I was on the other side, and every sort of other lie. For a long while her Majesty seemed completely to have forgotten me.

At last, Shōnagon tells us, a messenger arrived with a letter from the Small Palace. On opening it she found a single petal of the mountain-azalea, wrapped up in a sheet of paper. On the paper nothing was written, but on the petal were the words: 'My love, long silent....'[1]

Then to Shōnagon in her excitement the

[1] In allusion to the poem: 'Like a river that has dived into the earth, but is flowing all the while; so my heart, long silent, leaps up replenished in its love.'

Moreover, the azalea signifies silence because it is of the shade of yellow known as *kuchinashi* and *kuchi nashi* means 'mouthless,' 'dumb.'

strangest thing happened. When she sat down to write her reply she could not remember the first words of the poem to which she knew the Empress was alluding. Not to make some reference to these words would place her under a suspicion hardly less grave than that from which she seemed just to be emerging. To side with Michinaga was indiscreet; but to misunderstand a literary allusion was disgraceful. Fortunately a small boy who happened to be in the room heard Shōnagon fumbling for the elusive words and piped out: 'Like a river that has dived. . . .'

When I arrived, continues Shōnagon, describing her meeting with the Empress, I felt very nervous. . . . Her Majesty pretended not to know me and asked whether I was a new lady-in-waiting. Then turning to me she said: 'It was a bad poem that I made use of. But for a long time I had been feeling that something of the kind must be said. I am wretched all the time, when you are not here.' I could see at once that everything was right again. Presently I confessed that I had been in difficulties about the beginning of the poem, till a little boy told me how it went. She was very much amused. 'That is just what happens,' she said. 'It is always those old tags that slip one's memory. One grows careless about them. . . .'

The banishment of the Empress's brothers was not a very serious affair. Korechika paid a secret visit to the Capital in the late autumn of 996, and in the spring of 997 both brothers were officially recalled, in consequence of the general amnesty which celebrated the birth of the Empress Sadako's child.

In the summer of that year Sadako and her ladies returned to the Emperor's Palace, bringing with them the little princess Osako.

The following extract dates from 998:

While the western side-room was being got ready for the Continual Service, there were, of course, a lot of priests about, hanging up Buddhas and so on. Two days after this we heard a strange voice out on the veranda saying: 'There'll be some scraps left from the offerings, I suppose,' and one of the priests replied that it was too early yet to say. We wondered who it could be, and looking out saw an old nun, wearing an extraordinarily grimy pair of hunting-trousers, very narrow and short, and something in the nature of a cloak, that hardly came more than five inches below her belt and was as dirty as the trousers—the sort of garment, indeed, that is put on to a performing monkey. 'What is she saying?' I asked, and the old woman herself in a strange, affected voice croaked that she was a disciple of Buddha. 'I am only asking for the Lord Buddha's leavings,' she said. 'But these monks are stingy and won't give me any.' Her voice was refined and her speech that of someone who had moved in good society. I could not help feeling very sorry that a gentlewoman should have sunk to so miserable a plight. I said I supposed she never ate anything but Buddha's holy leavings, and said it was an edifying diet. She saw that I was laughing at her and cried out at once: 'Not eat anything else! I don't eat scraps from the altar, I can tell you, when I can get anything better!' We then put some fruit and some broad-cakes into a basket and sent them out to her. When she was feeling thoroughly comforted inside, she became very talkative. The young girls teased her with questions, asking whether she had a lover, and where her house was. Her replies were very lively, not to say scurrilous. Someone asked her whether she could sing and dance, which set her off on a long ballad about 'With whom shall I sleep to-night? With the sheriff of Hitachi will I sleep; for his skin is the best to touch.' There was a great deal more of it. This was followed by 'Many as the red leaves on the peak of Mount Otoko are the tongues that whisper my shame.' While she was singing, she rolled her head from side to side in the most extraordinary manner. We were now all getting rather tired of her. . . . Some said we ought to give her a present before we drove her away. The Empress heard this. 'I can't think what possessed you to let her make such a painful exhibition of herself,' her Majesty exclaimed. 'Her singing was really more than I could endure. I was obliged to stop up my ears. Here, take this cloak and send her off with it as quickly as you can.'

'Her Majesty sends you this cloak,' we told her. 'Your own is rather soiled; it would be nice if you were to put on something fresh.' We tossed it to her, and she received it with a profound bow; then threw it across her shoulders and executed a sort of dance. But we could not stand her a moment longer, and went indoors.

After this she got into the habit of coming, and was always trying in one way or another to call attention to herself. We used to call her 'the sheriff of Hitachi.' She still wore the same filthy cloak, and we wondered how she had disposed of the one we gave her. She had, indeed, long ceased to amuse us when one day Ukon, the Emperor's waiting-woman, came over to her Majesty's apartments and the Empress began telling her that we had taken up with this extraordinary old creature, who was always coming to the Palace. Then she made Kohyōye do her imitation of 'the sheriff of Hitachi.' 'Do show her to me one day,' cried Ukon; 'I long to see her. Don't think I shall run off with her. I quite realize that she is your perquisite.'

However, soon after this another nun, crippled but very well-behaved and respectable, called us out on to the veranda and begged for assistance. She seemed so ashamed of having to beg, that we were sorry for her. When we gave her some clothes, she did indeed prostrate herself profoundly, but in how different a manner from the other! Just as she was going off, with tears of gratitude in her eyes, 'Hitachi' turned up. She saw her, and was so jealous that she did not come near us again for ever so long afterwards.

A great friend of Sei Shōnagon's was Fujiwara no Yukinari, a first cousin of her chief lover, Tadanobu.

One day [1] when my lord Yukinari came to see us, he stayed for an immense while talking to someone outside. 'Who was it?' I asked, when he at last appeared. 'Ben no Naishi' (one of the Empress's gentlewomen), he replied. 'What can you have found to talk about with her, that took so long?' I asked, very much surprised. 'If the Clerk of the Grand Secre-

[1] 998, third month. Yukinari was then twenty-six. He died at the age of fifty-five, in 1027. Often called Kōzei.

tariat [1] had come along, you would soon have found yourself left in the lurch.' 'Now who, I should like to know, has told you about that business,' he said, laughing. 'As a matter of fact, that was what she was talking to me of just now. She was trying to persuade me not to tell anyone about it.'

Yukinari has no particular talents,[2] or indeed any characteristic likely to recommend him on a superficial acquaintance, and everyone else is content to take him as he seems. But I have had opportunities of seeing the deeper parts of his nature, and I know that he is far from being so ordinary as he appears. I have often said so to the Empress; and as a matter of fact, she knows it quite well herself. . . . But the young girls are always abusing him and openly repeating the most disagreeable stories about him. 'What a wretched sight he is!' they say. 'And why can't he recite the Scriptures and make

[1] This gentleman was evidently carrying on an affair with Ben no Naishi. There was a Clerk of the Left and a Clerk of the Right. The person referred to is either Minamoto no Yoriyoshi or Fujiwara no Tadasuke.

[2] A few years later Yukinari became known as the greatest calligrapher of his time.

poems like other prople? He is really very tiresome.'

The truth is, these ladies do not interest him and he never addresses a word to them. He always says: 'I wouldn't mind if a woman's eyes stood upright in her head, nor if her eyebrows spread all over her forehead and her nose were crooked, provided she had a good mouth and a fine chin and neck. A bad voice I couldn't, of course, stand.' 'But come to think of it,' he would add, 'faces are rather important. It *is* unpleasant when people are ugly.' This has added to the number of his enemies all ladies who believe themselves to have narrow chins or mouths that are lacking in charm, and it is they who have tried to prejudice her Majesty against him.

As it was I whom he first employed to carry messages to the Empress, he seems unable to communicate with her in any other way. If I am in my room he sends for me to the front of the house, or else comes right into our quarters. When I am not at the Palace but in my home, he follows me there and even if he has written a note [1] he brings it in himself, saying that if

[1] For the Empress.

anything prevents my going back to Court immediately, he will be obliged if I will send a messenger to her Majesty 'with instructions to report what he is now about to tell me,' and so forth. It is useless for me to point out that there are plenty of people in the Palace who would gladly give a message. He rejects one after another. Once, with the best intentions, I suggested that it is often a good thing to act according to circumstances, instead of making for oneself these hard-and-fast rules. But he said it came natural to him to live according to rule, and 'one can't change one's nature.' 'Don't stand on ceremony,' I answered. He did not see the allusion,[1] and laughing in a puzzled way, he said, 'I am afraid there has been a good deal of talk lately about our being so friendly. Well, suppose we are! I don't see anything to be ashamed of. I think, by this time, you might uncover your face, and so on.' 'I daren't,' I answered. 'I have heard how particular you are about the shape of people's chins, and mine is very ugly.' 'Is it really?' he asked seriously; 'I

[1] To the Analects of Confucius: 'If you are wrong, don't stand on ceremony with yourself, but change!' Yukinari thinks that Shōnagon is inviting him to take liberties with her.

had no idea of that. Perhaps after all you had better not let me see you.' After this I always covered my face on any occasion when he could possibly have seen me; but I noticed that he never looked my way, and it seemed clear that he had taken what I said about my own ugliness quite seriously.

One morning Shikibu no Omoto [one of the Empress's ladies] and I lay in the side-room (where we had slept that night) till the sun was well up. Suddenly we heard someone sliding back the door that leads into the main building, and there before us stood the Emperor and Empress! We were so much surprised that we simply lay helpless, while their Majesties stood by, laughing immoderately at our confusion. Presently they came across and stood half hidden behind the pile of rugs and cloaks (for we had buried ourselves head and all under our bedding), to watch the people going to and fro between the Palace and the guard-room. Several courtiers (not, of course, having the least idea who was inside the room) came to the window and saluted us. The Emperor was much amused and begged me not to give him away.

When their Majesties went back to the main building, the Empress said, 'Come along, both of you,' intending us to go on duty that minute. 'Do at least give us time to make up our faces!' I answered, and we stayed where we were. Later on, when Shikibu and I were still talking about their Majesties' visit, we became conscious of something swarthy which had suddenly loomed up close to the front door of our room, and was visible through a chink in our curtains, where one flap had got caught up upon the framework. We thought it was only Noritaka,[1] but on looking more closely we saw that the face was not the least like his.

With a good deal of laughing and scuffling, we began pulling the curtain back into its place; but before we had finished doing so, we realized that it was Yukinari who had been looking at us. This was very annoying, for I had made a point of his never seeing me. Shikibu was sitting with her back to him, so she came out of it all right. Stepping forward, he now said: 'This time I have really managed to

[1] Brother-in-law of Murasaki, authoress of *The Tale of Genji*.

see you completely.' 'We thought it was only Noritaka,'[1] I explained, 'and were careless. I must say that, for a person who is supposed to take no interest in women, you stared pretty hard.' 'Someone,' he answered, 'told me recently that there is a particular charm in women's faces just at the moment they wake from sleep; so I came along here this morning hoping to get a chance of peeping into one of the bedrooms. I was already watching you when their Majesties were here, but you did not notice me.' Presently he raised the curtains[2] and made as though to join us.

[The section which follows dates from 999, second month.]

When I was away from the Palace on holidays there were several Court gentlemen who used to come and visit us. This seemed to agitate the people of the house. I was, however, not at all sorry to see it put a stop to, for I had no very

[1] Presumably Noritaka was closely related to Shōnagon's companion.

[2] The ladies were dressing in an alcove curtained off from the rest of the room.

strong feeling about any of these visitors. But it was difficult without rudeness to be invariably 'not at home' to people who were calling repeatedly at all hours of the night and day; all the more so because, precisely with those whose visits were causing most scandal, my acquaintance was in reality very slight.

So this time I made up my mind not to let my whereabouts be generally known, but only to tell Tsunefusa,[1] Narimasa,[2] and a few others.

To-day Norimitsu came, and told me in the course of conversation that yesterday my lord Tadanobu had tried to find out from him where I was, saying that as I was Norimitsu's 'sister' [3] he must surely know my address. 'He was very

[1] Minamoto no Tsunefusa, 969-1023.

[2] Minamoto no Narimasa. This gentleman, together with Tsunefusa and Tadanobu, reappears in Murasaki's *Diary*. The three make music together at the time of the Empress Akiko's confinement (A.D. 1008); 'but not a regular concert, for fear of disturbing the Prime Minister.'

[3] In early Japanese poetry 'sister' means beloved. But at this period it indicated a platonic relationship and is often contrasted with words implying greater intimacy. Tachibana no Norimitsu was famous for his courage; he once coped single-handed with a band of robbers that had entered Tadanobu's house.

insistent,' Norimitsu said to me, 'but I was determined not to give you away. He refused to believe that I didn't know, and went on pressing me in a way that really made me feel very uncomfortable. Moreover, Tsunefusa was sitting near by, looking perfectly innocent and unconcerned, and I was certain that if I caught his eye I should inevitably burst out laughing. In the end I was obliged to choke my laughter by seizing upon a piece of sea-cloth[1] that was lying on the table and stuffing it into my mouth. Everyone must have thought me very greedy, and wondered what new delicacy I had found to devour between meals. But I managed all the same to avoid telling him anything. If I had laughed, it would of course have been fatal. In the end, he really thought I did not know. It was splendid. . . .!' I begged him to go on as he had begun, and for days afterwards heard no more about it.

But very late one night there was a tremendous banging on the front gate, enough to have woken a houseful of people at twice the distance. I sent someone to see what was the matter, and was told it was an Imperial Guards-

[1] An edible seaweed.

man 'with a letter from the Major of the Body-guard of the Left,' that is to say, from Nori-mitsu. Everyone in the house was in bed, so I took the letter close to the hall-lamp, and read: 'To-morrow is the last day of the Spring Reading in the Palace. If Tadanobu is there keeping the penance-day with their Majesties, he may easily ask me where you are, and if (in front of everyone) he insists upon my telling him, I certainly shall not be able to keep up the pretence that I do not know. May I tell him you are here? I certainly won't unless I have your permission to do so.'

I wrote no answer, but sent him a minute piece of seaweed,[1] wrapped up in paper.

Next time he called, Norimitsu said: 'He got me into a corner and went on at me about it all night. It is really very disagreeable to be pestered like that, and as you did not answer the letter in which I asked for your instructions. . . . But, by the way, I did receive a wrapper containing a piece of seaweed. No doubt in a moment of absent-mindedness. . . .'

[1] Meaning 'If you are tempted to speak, stuff seaweed in your mouth as you did last time.'

As if one could conceivably do such a thing by accident! He still could not in the least understand what I had meant, and evidently thought I had merely sent him a very mean and useless present. Irritated by his stupidity, I made no reply, but seizing the inkstand wrote on a scrap of paper the poem: 'If from the fishing-girl who dives beneath the waves the present of a rag you have received, surely she hints that to the world you should not tell in what sea-bed she hides.' [1]

'So Madam has started writing poems, has she?' he exclaimed. 'I, for one, shall not read them,' and scrunching up the piece of paper, he marched off.

So it came about that Norimitsu and I, who had always been such good friends and allies, were for a while rather cool towards each other. Soon, however, he wrote to me saying: 'I may have been to blame; but even if you don't wish to see me, I hope you do not regard our old alliance as altogether a thing of the past. That,

[1] An acrostic. There is a series of ingenious puns; for example, *me-kuwase* = 'to hint with a wink,' but also 'to cause to eat rag.'

after all, would mean the breaking of a good many promises. . . .'

It was a favourite saying of his that people never sent him poems so long as they liked him. 'It's a sure sign that they have turned against one,' he used to say. 'When you have made up your mind that you can bear me no longer, just send me one of those, and I shall know what to make of it.'

Despite this warning, Shōnagon sent him another acrostic poem. 'I don't suppose he ever read it,' she continues, 'and in any case he never answered. Soon afterwards he was promoted to the Fifth Rank and became Lieutenant-Governor of Tōtōmi; since when our friendship has come completely to an end. . . .'

The following dates from about the same time:

A Court lady, when she is on holiday, needs to have both her parents alive.[1] She will get on best in a house where people are always going in and out, where there is a great deal of con-

[1] Shōnagon's father died before she went to Court.

versation always going on in the back rooms, and where at the gate there is a continual clatter of horsemen. Indeed, she would far rather have too much noise than too little.

It is very annoying if one is living in some-one else's house and a friend comes from Court, either openly or in secret, just to ask how long one will be away or to apologize for not having written ('I did not even know you were on holiday . . .')—it is, as I say, extremely annoying, particularly if he is a lover, to have the owner of the house coming and making a scene ('very dangerous . . . at this time of night too,' and more in the same style) merely because one has opened the front door for a moment, to let the visitor in. Then later on: 'Is the big gate locked?' To which the porter grunts in an injured tone: 'There's someone here still. Am I to lock him in?' 'Well, lock up directly he goes,' says the landlord. 'There have been a lot of burglaries round here lately.' All of which is not very pleasant to overhear.

After this the master of the house is con-tinually poking out his head to see whether the visitor is still there, to the great amusement of the footmen whom the guest has brought with him. Most alarming of all is to hear these footmen doing an imitation of the landlord's voice. What a row there will be if he hears them!

It may happen that someone, who neither appears to be nor indeed is in any way a lover, finds it more convenient to come at night. In that case he will not feel inclined to put up with the churlishness of the family, and saying: 'Well, it *is* rather late; and as it seems to be such a business for you to open the gate ...' he will take his departure.

But if it is someone of whom the lady is really fond, and after she has told him again and again that she dare not receive him, he nevertheless goes on waiting outside her room till dawn; at which point the porter, who has during his nightly rounds continually lingered regretfully by the gate, exclaims in a tone intended to be heard: 'The morning's come' (as though such a thing had never happened before!) 'and that front gate has been ———[1]

---

[1] The adverb he uses (*raisō to*), evidently a very emphatic one, was a slang expression of the time, the exact meaning of which is uncertain.

open all night,' whereupon in broad daylight, when there is no longer any point in doing so, he locks the gate—all that sort of thing is very trying.

As I have said, with real parents of one's own, it would be all right. But step-parents can be a nuisance. One is always wondering how they will take things; and even a brother's house can be very tiresome in this way.

Of course, what I really like is a house where there is no fuss about the front gate, and no one particularly minds whether it is midnight or morning. Then one can go out [1] and talk to whoever it may be—perhaps one of the princes, or of the lords attached to his Majesty's service —sit all through a winter's night with the shutters open, and after the guest has gone, watch him make his way into the distance. If he leaves just at daybreak, this is very agreeable, particularly if he plays upon his flute as he goes. Then, when he is out of sight, one does not hurry to go to bed, but discusses the visitor with someone, reviews the poems he made, and so gradually falls to sleep.

[1] Out to the front of the house.

'I saw someone, who had no business here, in the corridor early this morning. There was a servant holding an umbrella over him. He was just going away. . . .' So I heard one of the girls say, and suddenly realized that it was to a visitor of mine that she was referring!

However, I really didn't know why she should describe him as 'having no business here.' As a matter of fact, he is only a *chige*,[1] a person of quite comfortable eminence, whom I have every right to know, if I choose.

Presently a letter came from the Empress, with a message that I was to reply instantly. Opening it in great agitation, I saw a drawing of a huge umbrella; the person holding it was entirely hidden, save for the fingers of one hand. Underneath was written the quotation: 'Since the morning when dawn broke behind the fringe of the Mikasa[2] Hills. . . .'

The whole affair was a trivial one, but her Majesty might easily have been cross about it, and when the letter came I was actually hoping that no one would mention the matter to her.

[1] A courtier not admitted on to the Imperial dais.
[2] Mikasa means 'Three Umbrellas.'

And now, instead of a scolding, came only this joke, which, though it humiliated me, was really very amusing. I took another piece of paper and drawing upon it the picture of a heavy rain-storm, I wrote underneath: 'It is a case of much cry and no rain.'

MASAHIRO

Everyone laughs at Masahiro.[1] It must really be very painful for his parents and friends. If he is seen anywhere with at all a decent-looking servant in attendance upon him, someone is sure to send for the fellow and ask him whether he can be in his senses, to wait upon such a master. Everything at his house is extremely well done and he chooses his clothes with unusually good taste; but the only result is to make people say: 'How nice those things would look on anyone else!'

It is true that he does sometimes talk in the most peculiar way. For example, he was sending home some things he had been using when on duty at the Palace and he called for *two* messengers. One came, saying that there was not more there than one man could easily carry. 'You idiot,' said

[1] A member of the Minamoto clan; afterwards Governor of Awa.

Masahiro, 'I asked for two messengers because there is someone else's things here as well as my own. You can't ask one man to carry two men's stuff, any more than you can put two pints into a one-pint pot.' What he meant no one knew; but there was loud laughter.

Once someone brought him a letter, asking for an immediate reply. 'What a moment to choose!' Masahiro cried. 'I can hear beans crackling on the stove. And why is there never either ink or brushes in this house? Someone must steal them. If it were something to eat or drink that got stolen, I could understand. . . .'

When the Emperor's mother, Princess Senshi, was ill, Masahiro was sent from the Palace to inquire after her. When he came back, we asked him what gentleman had been in waiting upon the Princess. 'So-and-so and so-and-so,' he said, mentioning four or five names. 'No one else?' we said. 'Oh yes,' answered Masahiro, 'there were others there, only they had gone away.'

Once when I happened to be alone he came up to me and said: 'My dear lady, I have something I must tell you about at once.' 'Well, what is it?' I asked. 'Something,' he said, 'that I have just heard one of the gentlemen say.' And coming quite close to my curtain: 'I overheard someone who instead of saying "Bring your body up closer to mine," said "Bring your five limbs [1] . . ." ' and he went off into fits of laughter.

Once on the second of the three Appointment nights [2] it fell to Masahiro to go round oiling the lamps. He rested his foot on the pedestal of a lamp-stand, and as it happened to have been recently covered with *yutan* [3] and was not yet dry, it stuck to him, and as soon as he started to move away the lamp-stand toppled over. So fast was the framework stuck to his stockinged foot, that the lamp banged along after him as he walked, causing a regular earthquake at each step.

The Palace roll-call [4] has a special charm. Those who are actually waiting upon his Majesty do not have to attend it, but are

[1] For 'five limbs' the speaker uses a pedantic Chinese expression, corresponding to a Latinism in English.

[2] When the New Year appointments were announced.

[3] Cloth soaked in sticky oil.

[4] As opposed to the barrack roll-calls.

checked off on the spot by officers who come from seat to seat. But the rest all come clattering out into the courtyard, pell-mell. In our quarters,[1] if one goes to that side and listens hard, one can actually hear the names, which must have caused a flutter in many a susceptible breast. . . . Some by their manner of answering win great approval, while on others very severe judgments are passed. When it is all over, the watchmen twang their bows, and there is another great clatter of shoes, among which is discernible the even heavier tread of the Chamberlain who is advancing to take up his position at the north-east corner of the balcony, where he kneels in the attitude called the High Obeisance, facing the Emperor's seat, while with his back to the watchmen he asks them who was there. . . . Sometimes, if for one reason or another a good many courtiers are absent, no roll-call is held, and when the head-watchman reports this, the Chamberlain generally asks him to explain the reason why there

[1] The ladies-in-waiting's quarters in the Empress's apartments, as opposed to their rooms in the less prominent parts of the Palace.

was no roll-call, and then retires. But when Masahiro is on duty he does not listen to what he is told, and if the young lords try to teach him his duties, flies into a temper, lectures them on the impropriety of omitting a roll-call, and is laughed at for his pains not only by these lords, but by the very watchmen whom he is rebuking.

On one occasion Masahiro left his shoes on the sideboard in the Royal pantry. Everyone who passed broke into exclamations of disgust and called upon the owner of the filthy things to take them away at once. It was very awkward, for though no one dared mention Masahiro's name, everyone knew they were his. 'Who do these things belong to? I haven't the least idea,' said the Chief Steward or someone of that kind. Suddenly Masahiro appeared, saying: 'Those dirty things are mine!' The fact that he had the face to come for them in person caused a fresh sensation.

Once when neither of the chamberlains was on duty and there was no one near the High Table, Masahiro took a dish of beans that was lying there and hiding behind the small partition,[1] began stealthily devouring them. Presently some courtiers came along and pulled away the partition. . . .

I have a great objection to gentlemen coming to the rooms of us ladies-in-waiting and eating there. Some gentlewomen have a tiresome habit of giving them food. Of course, if he is teased long enough and told that nothing can happen till he has eaten, a man will in the end give way. He cannot very well express disgust at what he is offered, cover up his mouth, or turn his head the other way. But for my part, even if they come very late and very drunk, I absolutely refuse to give them even so much as a bowl of rice. If they think this is mean, and don't come again—well then, let them not come!

Of course, if one is at home and food is sent from the back room, one cannot interfere. But it is just as unpleasant.

Elsewhere Shōnagon says:

The things that workmen eat are most extra-

[1] A movable partition which concealed the washing-place. On the inside was painted a cat; on the outside, sparrows and bamboos.

ordinary. When the roof of the eastern wing was being mended, there were a whole lot of workmen sitting in a row and having dinner. I went across to that side of the house and watched. The moment the things were handed to them, they gulped down the gravy, and then, putting their bowls aside, ate up all the vegetables. I began to think that they were going to leave their rice, when suddenly they fell upon it and in a twinkling it had all disappeared. There were several of them sitting there together and they all ate in the same way; so I suppose it is a habit of builders. I can't say I think that it is a very attractive one.

Another of Shōnagon's butts was Fujiwara no Nobutsune, Assistant in the Board of Rites.

'I am very ready at making Chinese poems or Japanese,' he said to her one day,[1] 'you need only give me a subject. . . .' 'That is easily done,' I said. 'It shall be a Japanese poem.' 'Good,' he cried. 'But you had better give me a whole lot, while you are about it. *One* would

[1] Summer, 998 (?).

hardly be worth while.' But when I gave him the subject, he suddenly lost his nerve and said he must be going. Someone told us it was his handwriting that he was uneasy about. 'He writes an atrocious hand in Chinese and Japanese,' this lady said, 'and he has been laughed at about it so much that he is apt to take fright.'

In the days [1] when he had an appointment in the Board of Household Works, he sent a plan to some craftsman or other with 'This is the way I want it done' written underneath in Chinese characters of a sort one would never have supposed anyone in the world could perpetrate. The document was such a monstrosity that I seized it and wrote in the margin 'I should not do it quite in this way, or you will indeed produce a queer object.' The document the went to the Imperial apartments, where it was passed from hand to hand, causing a good deal of amusement.

Nobutsune was very angry about this.

ANNOYING THINGS

When one sends a poem or a *kayeshi* ('return-

In 996.

poem') to someone and, after it has gone, thinks of some small alteration—perhaps only a couple of letters—that would have improved it.

When one is doing a piece of needlework in a hurry, and thinking it is finished unthreads the needle, only to discover that the knot at the beginning has slipped and the whole thing come undone. It is also very annoying to find that one has sewn back to front.

Once when her Majesty was staying at my Lord the Prime Minister's house,[1] and she was with him in the western wing, to which he had retired in order to make room for her, we gentlewomen found ourselves herded together in the central building with very little to occupy us. We were romping and idling in the corridors, when someone came from the Empress, saying: 'This dress is wanted in a hurry. Please get together and do it immediately. Her Majesty wants it back within the hour.'[2] What we were to make up was a piece of plain,

[1] The Minami no In, the palace of Michitaka, the Empress's father. This episode must have taken place in the twelfth month of 992.

[2] I.e. two hours, the Japanese hour being twice ours.

undamasked silk.[1] We all collected along the front of the main hall, the work was given out piecemeal, and there was a wild race to see who could get her bit finished first. It was a maddening business, for one was not near enough to some of the others to see what they were doing.

Nurse Myōbu got hers done in no time, and laid it down in front of her. She had been told to sew the shoulders of the bodice, but had carelessly put the stuff inside out and without finishing off the work in any way had just slammed it down and gone off to amuse herself. When we came to put the dress together, the back seams did not fit properly, and it was clear there had been some mistake. There was a great deal of laughing and scolding. It was clearly Myōbu's fault and everyone said she must do her seam over again.

'I should first like to know who has sewn anything wrong,' she burst out. 'If anyone had sewn a piece of damask inside out, so that the pattern was wrong, of course she would have to do it again. But with plain silk, what differ-

[1] Reading *hiraginu*.

ence can it make? If anyone has got to do it all over again, I should think it had better be one of the girls who did not do her share the first time.' 'How can anyone have the face to suggest such a thing?' the others cried. But Myōbu could not be prevailed upon, and in the end Gen Shōnagon and some others were obliged to unpick the stitches and put the thing right. It was amusing to watch the expression on their faces while they did so.

This all happened because her Majesty was to wait upon the Emperor at dusk and wanted the dress to be ready in time. 'I shall know that the one who gets her work done quickest really loves me,' she had said.

It is particularly annoying if a letter goes astray and gets delivered to someone to whom one would never have dreamt of showing it. If the messenger would simply say straight out that he has made a mistake, one could put up with it. But he always begins arguing and trying to prove that he only did as he was told. It is this that is so trying, and if there was not always someone looking on, I am sure I should rush at him and strike him.

To plant a nice *hagi* [1] or *susuki*,[2] and then find someone with a long-box and gardening tools who has dug them up and is carrying them away—is a painful and annoying experience. The provoking part of it is that if a male even of the humblest description were on the spot, the wretch would never dare to do so. When one stops him and expostulates, he pretends he has only thinned them out a bit, and hurries off. I really cannot tell you how annoying it is.

One is staying with a provincial Governor or some small official of that kind, and a servant comes from some grand house. He speaks and behaves with the utmost rudeness and an air as much as to say 'I know I am being rude; but people like you can't punish me for it, so what do I care?' I find that very annoying.

A man picks up a letter that one does not want him to see and takes it with him into the courtyard, where he stands reading it. At the first moment one rushes after him in rage and desperation; but at the curtains one is obliged to stop, and while one watches him reading one

[1] Lespedeza bicolor.　　　[2] Eularia japonica.

can hardly prevent oneself from swooping down upon him and snatching it away.

A lady is out of humour about some trifle, and leaving her lover's side goes and establishes herself on another couch. He creeps over to her and tries to bring her back, but she is still cross, and he, feeling that this time she has really gone too far, says: 'As you please,' and returns to the big bed, where he ensconces himself comfortably and goes to sleep. It is a very cold night and the lady, having only an unlined wrap to cover herself with, soon begins to suffer. She thinks of getting up; but everyone else in the house is asleep and she does not know what to do or where to go. If she must needs have this quarrel, it would have been better, she thinks, to start it a little earlier in the evening. Then she begins to hear strange noises both in the women's quarters and outside. She becomes frightened and softly creeps towards her lover, plucks at the bedclothes, and raises them. But he vexingly pretends to be fast asleep; or merely says: 'I advise you to go on sulking a little longer.'

Small children and babies ought to be fat.

So ought provincial governors, or one suspects them of being bad-tempered. As regards appearance, it is most essential of all that the boys who feed the carriage-oxen should be presentable. If one's other servants are not fit to be seen, they can be stowed away behind the carriage. But outriders or the like, who are bound to catch the eye, make a painful impression if they are not perfectly trim. However, if it is too obvious that one's menservants have been lumped together behind the carriage in order to escape notice, this in itself looks very bad.

It is a mistake to choose slim, elegant youths on purpose that they may look well as footmen, and then let them wear trousers that are grimy at the ends and hunting-cloaks or the like that have seen too much wear. The best that can be hoped is that people will think they are walking beside your carriage by chance and have nothing to do with you.

But it is a great convenience that all one's servants should be handsome. Then if they should happen to tear their clothes or make themselves in any way shabby or untidy, it is more likely to be overlooked.

Officers of State, who have official attendants allotted to them, sometimes spoil the effect by allowing their page-boys to go about dirty and ill-kempt.

Whether a gentleman is at home or on an official mission or staying with friends he ought always to have round him quantities of handsome page-boys.

For secret meetings summer is best. It is true that the nights are terribly short and it begins to grow light before one has had a wink of sleep. But it is delightful to have all the shutters open, so that the cool air comes in and one can see into the garden. At last comes the time of parting, and just as the lovers are trying to finish off all the small things that remain to be said, they are suddenly startled by a loud noise just outside the window. For a moment they make certain they are betrayed; but it turns out only to be a crow that cried as it flew past.

But it is pleasant, too, on very cold nights to lie with one's lover, buried under a great pile of bed-clothes. Noises such as the tolling of a bell sound so strange. It seems as though they came up from the bottom of a deep pit. Strange, too, is the first cry of the birds, sounding so muffled and distant that one feels sure their beaks are still tucked under their wings. Then each fresh note gets shriller and nearer.

VERY TIRESOME THINGS

When a poem of one's own, that one has allowed someone else to use as his, is singled out for praise.

Someone who is going a long journey wants introductions to people in the various places through which he will pass, and asks you for a letter. You write a really nice letter of recommendation for him to present to one of your friends who lives at some place through which he will pass. But your friend is cross at being bothered and ignores the letter. To be thus shown up as having no influence is very humiliating.

MISCELLANEOUS

There is nothing in the whole world so painful as feeling that one is not liked. It always seems to me that people who hate me must be suffering from some strange form of lunacy.

However, it is bound to happen, whether at Court or in one's home, that some people like one and some don't; which I find very distressing. Even for a child of the servant-class (and much more for one of good-breeding) it is very painful, after having always been petted at home, to find itself the object of a disapproving stare. If the girl in question has anything to recommend her, one thinks it quite reasonable that she should have been made a fuss of. But if she is without attractions of any kind, she knows that everybody is saying, 'Fancy anyone making a pet of a creature like that! Really, parents are very odd!' Yes, at home or at Court the one thing that matters is to be liked by everyone, from their Majesties downward!

Shōnagon elsewhere tells us that she used often to say to the Empress: 'I must always come first in people's affections. Otherwise, I would far rather be hated or even actually maltreated. In fact, I would rather die than be loved but come second or third.'

Writing is an ordinary enough thing; yet

how precious it is! When someone is in a far corner of the world and one is terribly anxious about him, suddenly there comes a letter, and one feels as though the person were actually in the room. It is really very amazing. And, strangely enough, to put down one's thoughts in a letter, even if one knows that it will probably never reach its destination, is an immense comfort. If writing did not exist, what terrible depressions we should suffer from! And if it is a relief to put down, once and for all, the things that have been weighing on one's mind, with a vague idea that the person in question may one day read what one has written, it is no exaggeration to say that the arrival of an answer can sometimes work like a real Elixir of Life!

The boys employed by magicians are extraordinarily clever. When their master is sent for to perform a ceremony of purification, these boys are expected to read the invocations,[1] and no one thinks anything of it. But to see them

---

[1] Which would be in Chinese, as these magicians worked according to a method deduced from the Chinese *Book of Changes*.

dash up at exactly the right moment, without a word from their master, and sprinkle cold water on the face of the patient, really makes one envious. I wish I could get hold of boys like that to wait upon me!

If one hears a servant girl say about anyone, 'He's an awfully nice gentleman,' one at once feels a slight contempt for the person in question. One would really think better of him if she abused him. Even a lady can lose by being too much praised in the wrong quarters; and, considering how much one is certain to suffer by being decried, it seems a pity that even the praise one gets should only do one harm!

NARINOBU

Captain Narinobu [1] is a son of His Highness the Reverend President of the Board of War. He is not only very handsome, but also exceedingly intelligent. How that poor daughter of Kanesuke's must have suffered at the time he broke with her, and she was obliged to go off with her father to Iyo, where he had been

[1] Minamoto no Narinobu (born A.D. 972) was a son of Prince Okihira (953–1041).

appointed Governor! One imagines her being due to start at dawn, and his coming to say good-bye the night before. I see him wrapped in a Court cloak, standing in the pale moon-light of dawn, as she must then have seen him for the last time.

In old days he used frequently to come and see me. He talked with considerable freedom, never hesitating to say the most disagreeable things about those of whom he disapproved.

There was in those days a certain gentle-woman of her Majesty's, rather a tiresome person who made a great fuss about her penances, and the like. She was known by her surname, which was Taira or something grand of that sort. But she had really only been adopted by these people, and among the other girls it was considered amusing always to refer to her by her original name.

She was not at all good-looking—this Taira girl—nor had she any other quality to recom-mend her. But she seemed entirely unaware of her defects and always pushed herself forward when there was company at the Palace, in a way that her Majesty particularly disliked,

though no one had the strength of mind to tell
her so. . . .

Once, when the Empress said that Shikibu
no Omoto and I were to sleep in her apartments instead of going back to our own room,
we settled down for the night in the southern
ante-room. After a while there was a tremendous
banging on our door. We decided it would be a
nuisance to have anyone coming in, and pretended to be asleep. But the knocking was
followed by violent shouting, and I heard her
Majesty say: 'Go and wake her up, one of
you. She is only pretending to be asleep.' The
'Taira' girl then came in and tried to wake me;
but she found that I was very fast asleep indeed,
and saying that if I would not stir she must open
the door herself, she went out and began a conversation with the visitor. I kept on thinking
she would come back, but midnight came and
still she did not appear. I was fairly certain that
the visitor was my lord Narinobu. . . .

Next morning she heard us talking in our
ante-room, and joining us, said to me: 'I do
think that when a man comes through such
storms of rain as there were last night, you

ought to treat him better. I know that he has been behaving very badly lately, and that you had almost lost sight of him. But I think you ought to forgive anyone who arrives with his clothes as wet as that.'

I cannot follow that line of argument. It seems to me that if a man who comes regularly every night is not put off even by a heavy shower of rain, that is something to his credit. But if, after absenting himself for weeks on end, he is fool enough to choose such weather as this for coming back, then all I can say is I would rather he showed more sense and less devotion. But I suppose that is a matter of taste.

The case is this. Narinobu likes sometimes to have dealings with a woman who has observed and reflected sufficiently to acquire a mind of her own. But he has many other attachments to keep up, not to mention his main responsibility, and it would be quite impossible for him to see me often. His object in choosing so atrocious a night for his visit was chiefly that other people might be impressed by his devotion and point out to me how much beholden I ought to feel. However, I suppose if he did not care for me at all, he would not think it worth while to indulge even in such stratagems as these.

When it is raining I fall into complete gloom, and even if only a few hours ago the sun was shining brightly I cannot in the least remember what things looked like when it was fine. Everything looks equally disagreeable, so that it makes no difference to me whether I am in the loveliest corner of the Palace arcades or in the most ordinary of houses; so long as it is raining I can think of nothing else but how long the rain is going to last.

But if anyone comes on a night when the moon is up and there is a clear sky, even if it is ten days, twenty days, a month, a year, yes, even seven or eight years since his last visit, I can look back with pleasure on his visit; and even if the place is not very convenient for meeting and one must be prepared for interruption at any moment—even if, at the worst, nothing more happens than a few remarks exchanged at a respectful distance— one feels that next time, if circumstances are favourable, one will allow him to stay the night.

THE STORM

Among 'deceptive things' Shōnagon mentions boating excursions and tells the following
story: The sun was shining brightly; so calm
was the lake that it looked as though it was
tightly covered from corner to corner with a
sheet of light green, glossy silk. Never can day
have seemed more safe. We young girls had
thrown off our mantles and were helping at the
oars (we had brought some lads to wait upon us
and manage the boat), and singing one song
after another—really the whole excursion was
so delightful we wished a thousand times that
the Empress or some of her family were with
us—when a violent gale sprang up, the lake all
of a sudden became terribly rough, and soon
our only thought was how to get into shelter as
quickly as possible. It seemed impossible that
this lake, whose waves now hung over us as we
rowed with all our might to the shore, was the
same that a little while ago had been so sleepy
and harmless.

When one thinks of it, to be in a boat at all
is a terrible thing! It is bad enough, even in
reasonably shallow water, to trust oneself to

such a conveyance; but where the water may be any depth—perhaps a thousand fathoms—to embark upon a thing loaded up with goods and baggage of all kinds, with only an inch or two of wood between oneself and the water! However, the low-class people who manage the boat do not seem to be in the least frightened, but run up and down unconcernedly in places where a single false step would lose them their lives.

Even the loading of a ship, when they bang down into the hold huge pine-trees two or three feet in circumference, sometimes half a dozen of them at a time, is an amazing thing. Rich people of course go in ships with cabins, and those who are lucky enough to be in the middle of the ship do not get on so badly. But those who are near the sides get very dizzy. It is extraordinary how little strength there looks to be in those things they call thongs, which keep the oars in place. If one of those were to snap, the oarsman would be drowned in a minute; yet they are always quite thin.

Our cabin was a very lovely one, with fringed curtains, double doors, and sliding shutters. Of course, it would not have done for it to be so heavy as the cabins on ships such as I have been talking about; but all the same, it was like a complete little house. What frightened me most was looking at the other ships. Those in the distance, scattered here and there across the waters, looked like the bamboo leaves that one sometimes makes into toy boats. When at last we got back into the harbour it was full of ships with lighted torches on board, a wonderful sight. How sorry one was for the people whom one saw toiling along in those very small rowing-boats that they call *hashi* ! ... I can understand why it is that some quite ordinary people absolutely refuse to go in boats. It is true that travelling on land is also very dangerous; but, whatever may happen, it is always some comfort to have firm ground under one's feet.

Pilgrimage to the Hasedera [1]

While they were seeing about our rooms, the carriage (from which the oxen had been unyoked) was pulled up to the foot of the log

[1] Temple of Kwannon, near Kyōto.

stairway by which one climbs up to the temple.
Young priests, with nothing but body-belts
under their cassocks, and those clogs they call
ashida on their feet, were all the while hurrying
up and down the stairway without seeming to
take any notice where they stepped, and reciting,
as they went, scraps of the *Sūtras* or stray verses
from the rhythmic portion of the *Abhidharma
Kośa*,[1] in a manner pleasantly appropriate to
such a place. Our own ascent of the steps was
very much less secure; indeed, we crept up at
the side, never daring to let go of the railings,
in places where these young priests walked as
comfortably as on a board-floor.

'Your rooms are ready; you can come at
once,' someone said to us, and providing over-
shoes for the whole party he led us in. The
place was already full of pilgrims; some, too
poor to buy new coats, were wearing them with
the lining outside, others in Court robes and
cloaks of Chinese brocade were decked out
with almost too obtrusive a splendour. The

[1] Translated by de la Vallée Poussin, Geuthner, 1923
seq.; a treatise by Vasubandhu, expounding the philosophy of
the Sarvāstivādins.

sight of so many soft-boots [1] and slippers shuffling along the corridor was very amusing, and indeed reminded me of the Emperor's apartments in the Palace.

Several young men who seemed thoroughly at home in the place (probably retainers attached to the temple) accompanied us, saying, 'Now up a few steps,' 'Now down!' and so on, to prevent us falling in the dark. There was another party (I don't know who they were) close behind us. Some of them tried to push past, but our guides asked them to stand back, saying we were a party from the Palace and they must keep clear of us. Most of them said 'Indeed!' and at once drew back. But there were others who took no notice and rushed on as though all they had come for was to see who could get to the chapel first. On the way to our rooms we had to pass between rows of people, and it was not very pleasant. But once arrived, we got a view right up to the centre of the altar.[2] The sight was so strangely moving that I wondered why I had

[1] Slipped on over one's outdoor boots, like the slippers worn in a mosque.

[2] Literally, the low rails in front of the altar.

allowed so many months to go by without once coming here; the old feeling had woken again within me.

The altar was not lit by the ordinary lamps of the outer chapel, but by lamps that pilgrims had laid as offerings within the shrine itself; and in this terrifying furnace of light the Buddha flashed and sparkled with the most magnificent effect. Priest after priest came up to the lectern in front of the altar and, holding up his scroll in both hands, read out his prayer.[1] But so many people were moving about that it was impossible to make out what any particular priest was saying. All we could catch was an occasional phrase, when one voice for a moment pressed up from among the rest, such as 'These thousand lamps . . . offered on behalf of . . .'; but the names one could not make out. While with the streamers of my dress hung back over my shoulders I was prostrating myself towards the altar, a priest came up, saying 'I have brought you these,' and I saw that he was carrying a bough of anise,[2] a courtesy which though

---

[1] The priests were employed to make dedications on behalf of their patrons.

[2] Used in the decoration of Buddhist altars.

merely pious in intention was very agreeable. Presently another priest came from the direction of the altar and said he had recited our prayers for us 'very well,' and wanted to know how long we were staying. We got him to tell us the names of some of the other people who were in retreat at the temple, and hardly had he left us when another priest came with braziers, food, and so on. Our washing-water was in a pot with a spout and our washing-tub had no handles! 'I have given your servants that cell over there,' the priest said; and he called them up one at a time to show them where they had been quartered. A recitation of the Scriptures was about to begin, and the temple bell was ringing. 'Ringing for our good,' so we felt, which gave us a great sense of security.[1]

Next door to us was an ordinary sort of man who all the while was quietly prostrating himself till his head bumped against the floor. I thought at first that he must be doing it for show. But it soon became apparent that he was

[1] Allusion not identified. Must be to a poem such as: 'In this mountain temple at evening when the bell sounds, to know that it is ringing for our good, how comforting the thought!'

completely absorbed in his devotions. How wonderful that anyone can go on like this hour after hour without falling asleep! When for a short time he rested from these devotions, we heard him reciting the *Sūtras* in a low voice, so that we could not hear what he was reading, but with a very solemn intonation. We were just wishing he would read a little louder, when he broke off, and we heard him sniffing, not loudly enough to be disagreeable, but gently and secretly. I wondered what sort of trouble he was in and longed that his prayers might be answered.

When we had been at the temple several days, the mornings became very quiet and uneventful. The gentlemen and boys in attendance upon us usually went off to visit one or other of the priests in his cell, and we were left with very little to amuse us. Then suddenly, from quite close at hand would come the sound of the conch-shell,[1] taking us always com-

---

[1] When the great scholar Moto-ori visited this temple in 1772 he was startled by the sudden noise of the conch-horn, blown at the hour of the Serpent (9 a.m.). At once there came into his mind this passage from *The Pillow Book* and

pletely by surprise. Or a messenger would come bringing an elegant *tatebumi* [1] or stuffs in payment for some ritual or service, and laying the things down, would shout for the temple-servants to come and take them away, shriller and shriller, till his voice echoed among the hills. Sometimes the din of the temple gongs would suddenly rise to an unwonted pitch, and in answer to our question as to what was afoot, they would mention the name of some great mansion, saying 'It is a service [2] for her Lady-ship's safe delivery.' An anxious time for my Lord. No wonder he could not rest content till the priests were at their task!

But all this applies only to ordinary times at

'the figure of Shōnagon seemed to rise up before me' (*Suga-gasa Nikki,* third month, seventh day). It is in this same temple that, in *The Tale of Genji,* Murasaki lays the scene of the meeting between Ukon and the long-lost Tamakatsura. The local people (Moto-ori tells us) had no idea that the characters in *Genji* were imaginary, and pointed out to him 'the tomb of Tamakatsura.'

1 A note folded up and twisted into an elaborate knot. In this case it would contain instructions for special services or prayers.

2 A *kyōge* or ritual for 'instruction and transformation' of evil influences.

the temple. At New Year, for example, there is a never-ending throng of sightseers and pilgrims, who cause so much disturbance that the services have often to be abandoned.

One evening a large party arrived from the City—so late that we were sure they were going to stay the night. Such tall screens were put up round their quarters that the little acolytes staggered under the weight of them. We could hear mats being flopped down, and everyone seemed to be scurrying about getting things in order. They were taken straight to their quarters and great rustling curtains were hung upon the railings that separated their rooms from the chapel-enclosure. People, evidently, who were used to being waited upon and made comfortable. Presently there was a great rustling of skirts, which gradually died away in the distance. It seemed to proceed from a party of elderly gentlewomen, very respectable and discreet. No doubt their services had been required only for the journey, and they were now going home. 'Don't be careless about fire,' we heard someone say, 'these rooms are very dangerous.' Among the party was a boy of seven or eight, rather spoilt and conceited we thought, judging from his voice. It amused us to hear him calling out for the valets and grooms, and carrying on long conversations with them. There was also a darling baby of three or thereabouts that we could hear gurgling to itself in the way that drowsy children do. We kept on hoping that the mother or someone else would call to the nurse by name; then we should have had some chance of guessing who the people were.

That night the services went on uninterruptedly till daybreak and the noise was so great that we got no sleep. After the *Goya*,[1] I dozed off for a while, but was soon woken by a sound of coarse, noisy chanting, that seemed intentionally to avoid any kind of beauty or holiness. We recognized the *Sūtra* as that of the Temple Patron.[2] These rough voices no doubt belonged to mountain-hermits from far away, and bursting in upon us thus unexpectedly, they were strangely moving. . . .

[1] The early service, at about 3 a.m.
[2] I.e. Kwannon, whose *sūtra* forms the 25th chapter of the *Hokkekyō*.

During retreats of this kind, or indeed whenever I am away from home, I do not find it sufficient merely to have grooms and servants with me. One needs several companions of one's own class, who are pleased by the same things as oneself—indeed, it is as well to bring with one as many friends as possible. There may among one's maids be some who are less tiresome than the rest. But on the whole one knows all their opinions too well.

Gentlemen appear to share my feelings about this question; for I notice they always make up an agreeable party beforehand, when they are going on pilgrimage to a temple. . . .

Often the common people who come to Hasedera show a gross lack of respect for the better sort of visitors, lining up in front of one's pew (*tsubone*) so close that they brush one with the tails of their coats. There comes on me sometimes a strong desire to make this pilgrimage, and then when I have braved the terrifying noise of the waters, struggled up the dangerous causeway, and pressed into my seat, impatient to gaze at last upon the glorious countenance of Buddha, it is exasperating to find my view barred by a parcel of common white-robed priests and country-people, swarming like caterpillars, who plant themselves there without the slightest regard for those behind them. Often, while they were performing their prostrations, I have come near to rolling them over sideways!

When very grand people come, steps are taken to keep a clear space in front of them. But, of course, for ordinary people they won't take the trouble to interfere. If one sends for some priest with whom one has influence and asks him to speak, he will sometimes go so far as to say, 'Would you mind making a little more room there, please?' But the moment his back is turned, it is as bad as before.

Shōnagon records that once when she was attending a great service at the Bodai Temple, someone sent her a note saying, 'Come back at once. I am very lonely.' 'As a matter of fact,' she tells us, 'I was at the moment so much worked up by what was going on around me, that I had quite made up my mind never to quit the place again (to become a nun); and I cared as little as old Hsiang Chung [1] whether people at home were waiting for me.

A Recitant [2] ought to be good-looking. It is only if it is a pleasure to keep one's eyes on him all the time that there is any chance of religious feeling (*tōtosa*) being aroused. Otherwise one begins looking at something else and soon one's attention wanders from what he is reading; in which case ugliness becomes an actual cause of sin.

(*Written later*)

The time has come for me to stop putting down ideas of this kind. Now that I am getting to be a good [3] age, and so on, it frightens me to discover that I ever wrote such blasphemous stuff. I remember that whenever any priest was

[1] A Chinese who became so completely absorbed in the *Tao Tê Ching* of Lao Tzu that he sat reading it on the edge of a river until (according to one version of the story) the spring floods carried him away.

[2] Of the Scriptures.

[3] *Yoroshi*, 'good,' is used by Shōnagon just as we use the word 'good' in such expressions as 'a good while ago,' etc. Aston (p. 116) did not understand this and completely mistranslates the sentence.

reported to be of particular piety I would rush off immediately to the house where he was giving his readings. If this was the state of mind in which I arrived, I see now that I should have done better to stay away.

Retired Chancellors . . . finding time lie heavy on their hands, often go once or twice to services of this kind. Soon the habit grows upon them, and they will come even in the hottest days of summer, vaunting conspicuous under-jackets and light purple or blue-grey trousers; and often one will see one of them there with a taboo-ticket [1] in his cap, apparently in the belief that the sanctity of the performance he is attending is such as to excuse him from any of the observances proper to this particular day. He bustles in, makes some remark to the holy man who is occupied with the service, but even while he is doing so continually casts back glances at some ladies who are just being deposited from their carriage,

[1] It was the anniversary of his father's death, or the like, and he should have remained strictly closeted at home. The 'taboo-ticket,' *mono-imi no fuda*, was worn as a sign that he must not be disturbed.

and indeed seems ready to take an interest in anything that turns up. Presently he discovers in the audience some friend whom he has not seen for a long time, and with many exclamations of astonishment and delight comes across and sits next to him. Here he chats, nods, tells funny stories, opens his fan wide and titters behind it, rattles a string of dandified beads, fiddles with his hands, and all the while looks round in every direction. He discusses what sort of carriages the people come in, finding fault with some and praising others, compares the services held recently at various houses— an Eight Recitations at so-and-so's, a Dedication of Scriptures given by someone else—and all this while he does not hear a word of what the priest is reading. And indeed, it would not interest him much if he did; for he has heard it all so often that it could no longer possibly make any impression upon him.

Stray Notes

One writes a letter, taking particular trouble to get it up as prettily as possible; then waits for the answer, making sure every moment that it cannot be much longer before something comes. At last, frightfully late, is brought in— one's own note, still folded or tied exactly as one sent it, but so finger-marked and smudged that even the address is barely legible. 'The family is not in residence,' the messenger says, giving one back the note. Or 'It is his day of observance and they said they could not take any letters in.' Such experiences are dismally depressing.

One has been expecting someone, and rather late at night there is a stealthy tapping at the door. One sends a maid to see who it is, and lies waiting, with some slight flutter of the breast. But the name one hears when she returns is that of someone completely different, who does not concern one at all. Of all depressing experiences, this is by far the worst.

Someone comes, with whom one has decided not to have further dealings. One pretends to be fast asleep, but some servant or person connected with one comes to wake one up, and pulls one about, with a face as much as to say 'What a sleep-hog!' This is always exceedingly irritating.

If someone with whom one is having an

affair keeps on mentioning some woman whom he knew in the past, however long ago it is since they separated, one is always irritated.

It is very tiresome when a lover who is leaving one at dawn says that he must look for a fan or pocket-book that he left somewhere about the room last night. As it is still too dark to see anything, he goes fumbling about all over the place, knocking into everything and muttering to himself, 'How very odd!' When at last he finds the pocket-book he crams it into his dress with a great rustling of the pages; or if it is a fan he has lost, he swishes it open and begins flapping it about, so that when he finally takes his departure, instead of experiencing the feelings of regret proper to such an occasion, one merely feels irritated at his clumsiness. . . .

It is important that a lover should know how to make his departure. To begin with, he ought not to be too ready to get up, but should require a little coaxing: 'Come, it is past daybreak. You don't want to be found here . . .' and so on. One likes him, too, to behave in such a way that one is sure he is unhappy at going and would stay longer if he possibly could. He should not pull on his trousers the moment he is up, but should first of all come close to one's ear and in a whisper finish off whatever was left half-said in the course of the night. But though he may in reality at these moments be doing nothing at all, it will not be amiss that he should appear to be buckling his belt. Then he should raise the shutters, and both lovers should go out together at the double-doors, while he tells her how much he dreads the day that is before him and longs for the approach of night. Then, after he has slipped away, she can stand gazing after him, with charming recollections of those last moments. Indeed, the success of a lover depends greatly on his method of departure. If he springs to his feet with a jerk and at once begins fussing round, tightening in the waist-band of his breeches, or adjusting the sleeves of his Court robe, hunting-jacket or what not, collecting a thousand odds and ends, and thrusting them into the folds of his dress, or pulling in his over-belt—one begins to hate him.

I like to think of a bachelor—an adventurous

disposition has left him single—returning at
dawn from some amorous excursion. He looks
a trifle sleepy; but, as soon as he is home,
draws his writing-case towards him, carefully
grinds himself some ink and begins to write his
next-morning letter—not simply dashing off
whatever comes into his head, but spreading
himself to the task and taking trouble to write
the characters beautifully. He should be clad
in an azalea-yellow or vermilion cloak worn
over a white robe. Glancing from time to time
at the dewdrops that still cling to the thin
white fabric of his dress, he finishes his letter,
but instead of giving it to one of the ladies who
are in attendance upon him at the moment, he
gets up and, choosing from among his page-
boys one who seems to him exactly appropriate
to such a mission, calls the lad to him, and
whispering something in his ear puts the letter
in his hand; then sits gazing after him as he
disappears into the distance. While waiting for
the answer he will perhaps quietly murmur to
himself this or that passage from the *Sūtras*.
Presently he is told that his washing-water and
porridge are ready, and goes into the back

room, where, seated at the reading-table, he glances at some Chinese poems, now and then reciting out loud some passage that strikes his fancy. When he has washed and got into his Court cloak, which he wears as a dressing-gown (without trousers), he takes the 6th chapter of the Lotus Scripture and reads it silently. Precisely at the most solemn moment of his reading —the place being not far away—the messenger returns, and by his posture it is evident that he expects an instant reply. With an amusing if blasphemous rapidity the lover transfers his attention from the book he is reading to the business of framing his answer.

One day when the Lord Abbot [1] was visiting his sister, the Mistress of the Robes, in her apartment, there came a fellow to her balcony, saying, 'A terrible thing has happened to me, and I don't know where to go and complain.' He seemed to be on the verge of tears. 'What is the matter?' we asked him. 'I was obliged to leave home for a little while,' he replied, 'and while I was away my miserable house was burnt to the ground. For days past I have been

[1] The Empress's brother, Ryū-en.

living on charity, squeezed into other people's houses, like a *gōna* [1] in an oyster-shell. The fire began in one of the hay-lofts belonging to the Imperial Stables. There is only a thin wall between, and the young lads sleeping in my night-room came near to being roasted alive. They didn't manage to save a thing.'

The Mistress of the Robes laughed heartily at this, and I, seizing a slip of paper, wrote the poem: 'If the sunshine of Spring was strong enough to set the royal fodder ablaze, how could you expect your night-room to be spared?' [2] I tossed this to him, amid roars of laughter on the part of the other gentlewomen, one of whom said to the man, 'Here's a present from someone who is evidently much upset at your house having been burnt down.' 'What's the use of a poem-slip to me?' he asked. 'It won't go far towards paying for the things I've lost.' 'Read it first!' said someone. 'Read it, indeed!' he said. 'I would gladly, if I knew so

[1] A creature that squeezes its way into the shells of other fish.

[2] There is here a series of puns too complicated for explanation.

much as half a letter. ...' 'Well then, get someone to read it to you,' said the same lady. 'The
Empress has sent for us and we must go to her
at once. But with a document such as that in
your hands, you may be certain that your
troubles are over.' At this there were roars of
laughter. On our way to the Empress's rooms,
we wondered whether he really would show it
to anyone, and whether he would be very
furious when he heard what it was.

We told her Majesty the story, and there was
a lot more laughing, in which the Empress
joined. But she said afterwards that we all
seemed to her completely mad.

PRETTY THINGS

The face of a child that has its teeth dug into
a melon.

A baby sparrow hopping towards one when
one calls 'chu, chu' to it; or being fed by its
parents with worms or what not, when one has
captured it and tied a thread to its foot.

A child of three or so, that scurrying along
suddenly catches sight of some small object
lying on the ground, and clasping the thing in

its pretty little fingers, brings it to show to some grown-up person.

A little girl got up in cloister-fashion [1] tossing back her head to get the hair away from her eyes when she wants to look at something.

CHILDREN

A child of four or five comes in from a neighbour's house and gets into mischief, taking hold of one's things, throwing them about all over the room, and perhaps breaking them. One keeps on scolding the creature and pulling things out of its hands, and at last it is beginning to understand that it cannot have everything its own way, when in comes the mother, and knowing that it will now get its way the child points at something that has taken its fancy, crying 'Mama, show me this!' and tugs at the mother's skirts. 'I am talking to grown-up people,' she says, and takes no more notice. Whereupon the child, after pulling everything about, finally extracts the object it coveted. At this the mother just says 'Naughty!'

[1] What we should call bobbed hair; standing out fan-wise behind, and worn about six inches long over the temples.

without making any attempt to take the thing away and put it into safety; or perhaps, 'Don't do that; you're spoiling it,' but evidently more amused than angry. One dislikes the parent as much as the child. It is indeed agonizing to stand by and see one's possessions submitted to such treatment.

Among 'embarrassing things,' Shōnagon mentions 'An unpleasant-looking child being praised and petted by parents who see it not as it is but as they would like it to be. Having to listen while its parents repeat to one the things the child has said, imitating its voice.'

And again, 'Sometimes when in the course of conversation I have expressed an opinion about someone and perhaps spoken rather severely, a small child has overheard me and repeated the whole thing to the person in question. This may get one into a terrible fix. . . .'

I have the same feeling if someone is telling me a sad story. I see the tears in his eyes and do indeed agree that what he says is very sad; but somehow or other my own tears will not flow. It is no use trying to contort one's face into an expression of woe; in fact, nothing is any good.

Of the gentlewomen's apartments attached to the Empress's own quarters, those along the Narrow Gallery are the most agreeable. When the wooden blinds [1] at the top are rolled up, the wind blows in very hard, and it is cool even in summer. In winter, indeed, snow and hail often come along with the wind; but even so, I find it very agreeable. As the rooms have very little depth and boys, [2] even when so near to the Imperial apartments, do not always mind their manners, we generally ensconce ourselves behind screens, where the quiet is delightful, for there is none of the loud talk and laughter that disturb one in other quarters of the Palace.

I like the feeling that one must always be on the alert. And if this is true during the day, how much more so at night, when one must be prepared for something to happen at any moment. All night long one hears the noise of footsteps in the corridor outside. Every now

[1] Like our Venetian blinds.
[2] Bringing messages from home, or the like.

and then the sound will cease in front of some particular door, and there will be a gentle tapping, just with one finger; but one knows that the lady inside will have instantly recognized the knock. Sometimes, this soft tapping lasts a long while; the lady is no doubt pretending to be asleep. But at last comes the rustle of a dress or the sound of someone cautiously turning on her couch, and one knows that she has taken pity on him.

In summer she can hear every movement of his fan, as he stands chafing outside; while in winter, stealthily though it be done, he will hear the sound of someone gently stirring the ashes in the brazier, and will at once begin knocking more resolutely, or even asking out loud for admittance. And while he does so, one can hear him squeezing up closer and closer against the door.

In the fifth month I love driving out to some mountain village. The pools that lie across the road look like patches of green grass; but while the carriage slowly pushes its way right through them, one sees that there is only a scum of some strange, thin weed, with clear, bright water underneath. Though it is quite shallow, great spurts fly up as our horsemen gallop across, making a lovely sight. Then, where the road runs between hedges, a leafy bough will sometimes dart in at the carriage window; but however quickly one snatches at it, one is always too late.

Sometimes a spray of *yomogi* will get caught in the wheel, and for a moment, as the wheel brings it level, a delicious scent hovers at our window.

I love to cross a river in very bright moonlight and see the trampled water fly up in chips of crystal under the oxen's feet.

In the second month something happens in the Hall of the Grand Council. I really don't know exactly what it is, but they call it the Tests.[1] About the same time there is a thing they call the Shakuden. I believe it is then that they hang up Kuji [2] and the rest. They also

---

[1] The examinations for officers of the Sixth Rank and under.

[2] I.e. Confucius. This is the ceremony in honour of Confucius and his disciples. In Chinese, *Shih-tien*. I quote this passage because it illustrates the extraordinary vagueness of the women concerning purely male activities.

present something called the Sōmei to the Emperor and Empress. It comes in a stone pot and includes some very queer stuff.

People value sympathy more than anything in the world. This is particularly true of men; but I do not exclude women. One always regrets an unkind remark, even if it was obviously quite unintentional; and it is easy, without entering very deeply into someone else's sorrow, to say 'How unfortunate!' if the situation is indeed unfortunate, or 'I can imagine what he is going through,' if the person in question is likely to be much perturbed. And this works even better if one's remark is made to someone else and repeated than if it is heard at first hand.

One ought always to find some way of letting people know that one has sympathized. With one's relations and so on, who expect fond inquiries, it is difficult to get any special credit. But a friendly remark to someone who sees no reason to expect it is always certain to give pleasure. This all sounds very easy and obvious; but surprisingly few people put it into practice. It seems as though people with nice feelings must necessarily be silly, and clever people must always be ill-natured, men and women too. But I suppose really there must be lots of nice, clever people, if only one knew them.

Features that one particularly likes continue to give one the same thrill of pleasure every time one looks at a face. With pictures it is different; once we have seen them a certain number of times, they cease to interest us; indeed, the pictures on a screen that stands close to your usual seat, however beautiful they may be, you will never so much as glance at!

Again, an object (such as a fan, mirror, vase) may be ugly in general, but have some particular part which we can look at with pleasure. Faces do not work like this; they affect us disagreeably unless they can be admired as a whole.

[*Plan for a Story*]

A young man, who has lost his mother. The father is very fond of him, but marries again. The stepmother is very disagreeable, and the young man ceases to have any dealings with her part of the house. There is a difficulty about his clothes; they have to be mended by his old nurse or perhaps by a maid who used to be in the mother's service. He is given quarters in one of the wings, as though he were a guest, with pictures on the screens and panels, by first-rate masters too. At Court he cuts a very good figure and is liked by everyone. The Emperor takes quite a fancy to him and is always sending for him to join in concerts and so on. But the young man is always depressed, feels out of place, and discontented with his mode of life. His nature must be amorous to the verge of eccentricity. He has an only sister, married to one of the highest noblemen in the land, who dotes upon her and gratifies her every whim. To this sister the young man confides all his thoughts, finding in her society his greatest consolation.

THINGS THAT MAKE ONE HAPPY

Getting hold of a lot of stories none of which one has read before.

Or finding Vol. 2 of a story one is in a great state of excitement about, but was previously only able to secure the first volume. However, one is often disappointed.

To pick up a letter that someone has torn up and thrown away, and find that one can fit the pieces together well enough to make sense.

When one has had a very upsetting dream and is sure it means that something disagreeable is going to happen, it is delightful to be told by the interpreter [1] that it does not signify anything in particular.

THINGS THAT GIVE ME AN UNCOMFORTABLE FEELING

A child that has been brought up by a nasty foster-mother. Of course, this is not its fault. But somehow one always thinks of its connexion with such a person as a disagreeable quality in the child itself. 'I can't understand why it is' (says the foster-mother to the father of the child) 'that you should be so fond of all the other young gentlemen, and yet seem to take no trouble about this child and even to hate the sight of it.'

She speaks in loud tones of indignation. Probably the child does not understand exactly

[1] I.e. dream-interpreter. Modern experts have seldom been known to take this reassuring view.

what is being said; but it runs to the woman's knees and bursts into tears.

Another thing that makes me feel uncomfortable is when I have said I do not feel well and some girl of whom I am not very fond comes and lies by me, brings me things to eat, pities me, and without any response on my part, begins following me about and continually coming to my assistance.

TOOTHACHE

A girl of seventeen or eighteen with very beautiful hair, which she wears down her back, spreading in a great, bushy mass; she is just nicely plump, and has a very pale skin. One can see that she is really very pretty; but at the moment she has toothache very badly, her fringe is all drabbled with tears and (though she is quite unconscious of the fact) her long locks are dangling in great disorder. Her cheek, where she has been pressing it with her hand, is flushed crimson, which has a very pretty effect.

ILLNESS

It is the eighth month. A girl is wearing an unlined robe of soft white stuff, full trousers,

and an aster [1] mantle thrown across her
shoulders with very gay effect. But she has
some terrible malady of the chest. Her fellow
ladies-in-waiting come in turns to sit with her,
and outside the room there is a crowd of very
young men inquiring about her with great
anxiety: 'How terribly sad!' 'Has she ever had
such an attack before?' and so on. With them
no doubt is her lover, and he, poor man, is
indeed beside himself with distress. But as
likely as not it is a secret attachment, and,
fearful of giving himself away, he hangs
about on the outskirts of the group, trying
to pick up news. His misery is a touching
sight.

Now the lady binds back her beautiful long
hair and raises herself on her couch in order to
spit, and harrowing though it is to witness her
pain, there is even now a grace in her move-
ments that makes them pleasurable to watch.
The Empress hears of her condition and at
once sends a famous reciter of the Scriptures,
renowned for the beauty of his voice, to read at
her bedside. The room is in any case very small,

[1] Light purple, lined with clear blue.

and now to the throng of visitors is added a number of ladies who have simply come to hear the reading. It is impossible to accommodate them all behind the screens-of-state. At this exposed bevy of young women the priest constantly glances while he reads, for which he will certainly suffer in the life to come.

A house with tall pine-trees all round it. The courtyards are spacious, and as all the *kōshi* [1] are raised, the place has a cool, open look. In the main room there is a four-foot screen, with a hassock in front of it, on which is seated a priest about thirty years old or a little more. He himself is by no means ill-looking; but what strikes one most is the extreme elegance of his brown robe and mantle of thin lustrous silk. He is reciting the spells of the Thousand-Handed One, fanning himself meanwhile with a clove-dyed fan.

Within must lie a person gravely afflicted by some kind of possession; for presently there edges her way out from the inner room a rather heavily built girl, who is evidently going to act

[1] Partitions made of thin pieces of wood, laid trellis-wise.

as 'medium.' [1] She has fine hair, and is undeniably a handsome creature. She is dressed in an unlined robe of plain silk and light-coloured trousers. When she has seated herself in front of a little three-foot screen placed at right-angles to that of the priest, he wheels round and puts into her hand a minute, brightly polished rod. Then in sudden spasms of sound, with eyes tightly shut, he reads the Spell, which is certainly very impressive. A number of gentlewomen have come out from behind the curtains and stand watching in a group.

Before long a shiver runs through the medium's limbs and she falls into a trance. It is indeed extraordinary to watch the priest at work and see how stage by stage his incantations take effect. Behind the medium is . . . a slim boy in his teens (perhaps her brother) with some of his friends. From time to time they fan her. Their attitude is quiet and reverent; but if she were conscious, how upset she would be to expose herself thus in front of

[1] The incantations of the priest cause the spirit which is possessing the sick person to pass into the medium, who, being young and healthy, easily throws it off.

her brother's friends! Though one knows that she is not really suffering, one cannot help being distressed by her continual wailing and moaning. Indeed, some of the sick woman's friends, feeling sorry for the medium, creep up to the edge of her screen and try to arrange her disordered clothing in a more decent way.

After a while it is announced that the sick woman is somewhat better. Hot water and other necessaries are brought along from the back of the house by a succession of young maids, who, tray in hand, cannot forbear to cast a hurried glance in the direction of the holy man. . . . At last, at the hour of the Monkey (4 p.m.), having reduced the possessing spirit to an abject condition, the priest dismisses it. On coming to, the medium is amazed to find herself outside the screen, and asks what has been happening. She feels terribly ashamed and embarrassed, hides her face in her long hair, and glides swiftly towards the women's quarters. But the priest stops her for a moment, and, having performed a few magic passes, says to her, with a familiar smile that she finds very disconcerting, 'That's right! Now you're quite yourself again, aren't you?' Then he turns to the others and says: 'I would stay a little longer, but I am afraid I am at the end of my free time. . . .' He is about to leave the house; but they stop him, crying: 'We should like so much to make an offering. Perhaps you would tell us. . . .' He takes no notice and is hurrying away, when a lady of good birth, possibly one of the daughters of the house, comes up to the curtains that screen off the women's quarters and bids her servants tell the holy man that, thanks to his merciful condescension in visiting the house, the sick woman's sufferings had been much relieved, for which they all wished to thank him from the bottom of their hearts. Would he have time to come again to-morrow? 'The disorder,' says he, 'is of a very obstinate nature, and I do not think it would be safe to leave off. I am very glad that what I have done has already had some effect.' And without another word he goes away, making everyone feel as though the Lord Buddha himself had been with them in the house.

In the eighth month of 998, at the time of her second confinement, the Empress went to

stay with Taira no Narimasa,[1] the Superintendent of her Household, bringing with her
Princess Osako, her first child. The Imperial
Litter, writes Shōnagon, was carried in at the
east gate, which had been rebuilt on purpose.
But we ladies were driven round to the small
north gate. We did not think there would be
anyone on duty at the guard-house, and some
of us had let our hair get into great disorder.
We had, indeed, taken for granted that we
should be brought right up to the house itself,
so that it would not matter if we arrived rather
untidy. Unfortunately the gate was so small
that our carriages, with their high awnings,
could not go through. Matting was laid down
for us from here to the house, and in a very bad
temper we all got out and walked. So far from
being deserted, the guard-house was full of
courtiers and servants, who stared in a way that
was very annoying. I told the Empress about
this and she said, laughing, 'There are people
here too with eyes in their heads! I do not know
why you should suddenly become so careless.'
'But we had the carriages all to ourselves,' I

[1] Not to be confused with Minamoto no Narimasa,
mentioned above.

said, 'and it would have seemed very odd if we had begun fussing about how we looked. Any way, at a house such as this surely all the gates ought to be big enough to admit a carriage! I shall make fun of him about it when he comes.' At this moment Narimasa did indeed arrive, carrying an inkstand, which he begged me to accept for her Majesty's use. 'We are not best pleased with you,' I said. 'Why do you live in a house with such small gates?' 'I am a person of small importance,' he answered, smiling, 'and my gates are built to match.' 'Is there not a story about someone who increased the height of his gate?' I asked. This seemed to surprise him. 'I know what you are thinking of,' he said. 'The story of Yü Ting-kuo. But pardon me, I thought that only musty old scholars knew of such things. Even I should not have understood you, did I not happen to have strayed a little in those paths myself.' [1] 'Paths indeed!' I

---

[1] The story of Yü Kung, who rebuilt his gate because of a conviction that his son Ting-kuo would rise to greatness, is told in the little handbook of improving anecdotes to which I refer below (p 151). Shōnagon is laughing at the fact that Narimasa should so easily have been impressed.

exclaimed. 'I do not think much of your paths. The matting got buried in them and we fell about in every direction. An appalling scene. . . .'

'There has been a lot of rain,' he said. 'I am sure you did. Well, well; you'll be saying something else unpleasant in a minute. I am going,' and off he went. 'What happened?' asked the Empress. 'You seem to have frightened Narimasa away.' 'Oh no,' I said. 'I was only telling him how we could not get through the north gate.' Then I went to my own room.

I shared it with several of the younger girls. We were all so tired that we did not bother about anything, and went straight to sleep. Our room was in the east wing, and had a sliding door leading into the passage under the eaves at the back of the building. The bolt of this door was missing, but we did not notice it. Our host, however, who was naturally familiar with the peculiarities of the house, presently came to the door, and, pushing it open an inch or two, said in a queer, hollow voice: 'May one venture?' This he repeated several times. I opened my eyes, and there he was, standing behind a chink that was now about five inches wide. No doubt about who it was, for he happened to be in the full glare of a lamp we had put behind our screen. It was really very funny. In an ordinary way he was the last person in the world to take liberties; but he apparently had some curious idea that having the Empress in his house entitled him to treat the other guests as he pleased. 'Look what is there!' I cried, waking the girl next to me. 'Would you ever have expected it?' At this they all raised their heads, and, seeing him still standing at the door, burst into fits of laughter. 'Who goes there?' I challenged him at last. 'Show yourself!' 'It's the master of the house,' he answered, 'come to have a word with the lady in charge.' 'It was your gate I complained of,' I said. 'I never suggested that our door needed attention.' 'Yes, yes,' he answered, 'it is just that business of the gate that I have come about. Might I venture for one moment. . . .?' 'No, of course he cannot,' said all the girls in chorus. 'Just look at the state we are in!' 'Ah well, if there are young persons [1] . . .' and he disap-

[1] Shōnagon was now about thirty-four; Narimasa was fifty.

peared, closing the door behind him, amid loud laughter.

Really, if a man finds the door open, the best thing he can do is to walk in. If he solemnly announces himself he can hardly expect encouragement.

Next day when I was with the Empress I told her about this. 'It sounds very unlike him,' she said, laughing. 'It must have been your exploit yesterday (the allusion to the story of Yü Kung) that interested him in you. But he is a kind fellow, and I am sorry you are always so hard upon him.'

Her Majesty had been giving orders about the costumes for the little girls who were to wait upon Princess Osako. Suddenly (and this time I really think one could hardly be expected not to smile) Narimasa came to ask whether her Majesty had decided—what colour the facings of the children's vests were to be! He was also worried about the Princess's meals. 'If they are served in the ordinary way,' he said, 'it won't look well. To my mind, she ought to have a *tayny*[1] platter and a *tayny* dish-stand. . . .' 'And

---

[1] He uses an affected pronunciation.

be waited upon by the little girls for whom you have designed such lovely underclothes,' I added. 'You should not laugh at Narimasa,' the Empress said to me afterwards. 'I know everyone does it; but he is such a straightforward, unpretentious creature . . .' and I was glad of this scolding.

One day when I was with her Majesty and nothing particular was going on, someone came and said that the Superintendent wished to see me. Her Majesty overheard this and said, laughing: 'I wonder how he means to make a butt of himself this time! You'd better go and see.' I found him waiting for me outside. 'I mentioned that unfortunate business about the gate to my brother Korenaka,' he said, 'and he thought it was very serious. "I should advise you to obtain an interview with the lady at an hour when she has leisure to discuss the matter in all its bearings." That was what my brother advised.'

How very interesting! I was wondering whether he would not make some reference to his strange visit the other night. But he merely added: 'So I trust you will allow me to wait upon you in your room. At some spare moment when you have nothing better to do . . .' and with a bow he took his leave.

When I went back into the room the Empress asked me what was the matter. I told her what he had said, adding: 'I don't understand why he sent for me, specially when I was on duty too. Surely he might have come round to my room later on.' 'He thought,' replied the Empress, 'that it would give you pleasure to hear what a respect Korenaka has for you; that is why he was in a hurry to tell you. You must remember that Korenaka is a tremendous figure in his eyes.' She looked so charming while she was saying this!

Three months later, the Empress's second child, Prince Atsuyasu,[1] was born. In the second month of the next year (A.D. 1000) she was raised to the rank of Imperial Consort, that is to say, was made of equal importance with the Emperor himself, having previously been merely a sort of chief Queen. In the fourth month she returned to the Palace, and in the eighth fell seriously ill.

[1] Died in 1018, at the age of nineteen.

Meanwhile the Emperor's attention was concentrated chiefly upon his new concubine, Akiko (daughter of the Prime Minister, Michinaga), who had arrived at the Palace just a year ago, at the age of eleven.

Speaking of this time, the *Eigwa Monogatari* (Chapter 7) contrasts the gloom of the sick Empress's quarters with the scenes of winter-carnival that went on in the Emperor's apartments.

'Certain princes, still faithful to the Empress, came constantly to inquire after her, and in conversation with her ladies-in-waiting described how the *gosechi* festival had been kept in various great houses of the Capital. These gentlemen were received by Sei Shōnagon or some other of her Majesty's ladies.'

On the 29th day of the twelfth month (A.D. 1000) the Empress Sadako died, having a few hours previously given birth to a daughter the Princess Yoshiko.

What became of Sei Shōnagon after her mistress's death we do not know. We hear no more of her till 1009, when Murasaki Shikibu, author of *The Tale of Genji*, writes in her *Diary*: 'Sei Shōnagon's most marked characteristic is her extraordinary self-satisfaction. But examine the pretentious compositions in Chinese script which she scatters so liberally over the Court, and you will find them to be a mere patchwork of blunders. Her chief pleasure consists in shocking people; and as each new eccentricity becomes only too painfully familiar, she gets driven on to more and more outrageous methods of attracting notice. She was once a person of great taste and refinement; but now she can no longer restrain herself from indulging, even under the most inappropriate circumstances, in any outburst that the fancy of the moment suggests. She will soon have forfeited all claim to be regarded as a serious character, and what will become of her when she is too old for her present duties I really cannot imagine.'

And what did become of her? There is a tradition (*Kojidan*, vol. ii) that when some courtiers were out one day they passed a dilapidated hovel. One of them mentioned a rumour that Sei Shōnagon, a wit of the last reign, was now living in this place. Whereupon an incredibly lean hag shot her head out of the door, crying: 'Won't you buy old bones?' This, if we are to accept the story, was the last of Shōnagon's famous 'literary allusions'; for there is here a reference to the story of Kuo Wei, who maintained that there were racehorses so precious that even their bones were worth procuring.

There is, too, in the *Zoku Senzaishū* (Book 18) a poem sent by Shōnagon 'when she was old and living in retirement to someone who tried to visit her':

Tou hito ni	If to those who visit me
'Ari' to wa e koso	'She is at home'
Ii-hatene	I cannot bring myself to say
Ware ya wa ware to	Do not wonder, for often in consternation
Odorokare-tsutsu.	I ask myself whether I am I.

The character of Shōnagon appears in her book as a series of contradictions. She is desperately anxious not merely to be liked, but to occupy the foremost place in the affections of all whom she knows. Yet her behaviour, as she

herself records it, seems consistently calculated
to inspire fear rather than affection. Again, she
seems at some moments wholly sceptical, at
others profoundly religious; now unusually
tender-hearted, now egotistical and cold. Yet
all this does not imply that her character was in
reality complicated to an unusual degree, but
comes from the fact that she reveals herself to
us entirely and, as it were, from every facet,
whereas most writers of diaries and the like,
however little conscious intention they may
have of publishing their confessions, instinc-
tively present themselves always in the same
light. Her detachment about herself is paralleled
by a curious aloofness from all the associated
emotions of a scene, so that she can describe a
sick-bed as though it were a sunset, without
the slightest attempt to arouse pity, or for that
matter the least fear of provoking disgust.

Perhaps the strongest impression we get is
of her extreme fastidiousness and irritability,
which must have made her a formidable companion. She probably got on better with the
Empress than with anyone else because her
reverence for the Imperial Family compelled

her in the August Presence to keep her nerves in check.

As a writer she is incomparably the best poet of her time, a fact which is apparent only in her prose and not at all in the conventional *uta* for which she is also famous. Passages such as that about the stormy lake or the few lines about crossing a moonlit river show a beauty of phrasing that Murasaki, a much more deliberate writer, certainly never surpassed. As for Shō-nagon's anecdotes, their vivacity is apparent even in translation. Neither in them nor in her more lyrical passages is there any hint of a search for literary effect. She gives back in her pages, with apparently as little effort of her own as a gong that sounds when it is struck, the whole warmth and glitter of the life that sur-rounded her; and the delicate precision of her perceptions makes diarists such as Lady Anne Clifford (whose name occurs to me at random) seem mere purblind Hottentots.

This gift manifests itself incidentally in her extraordinary power of conveying character. Yukinari, Masahiro and Narimasa, despite their uniform absurdity, live with extraordinary distinctness; as does the Empress herself, the only other woman whom the authoress allows to figure in her pages.

Her style is very much less 'architected' than Murasaki's; but there are moments when she begins building up a huge network of dependent clauses in a manner extremely close to *Genji*, and often one feels that the earlier book leads us, so to speak, to the brink of the other. This fits in with the presumed dates. *Genji* was probably begun in 1001, when Murasaki lost her husband, and the *Pillow-Book* seems, with the possible exception of two or three entries, to have been written before the twelfth month of 1000, when the Empress Sadako died.

Shōnagon has often been spoken of as learned. Our only source of information on the subject is her own book. In it she shows signs of having read the *Mēng-ch'iu*, a collection of edifying Chinese anecdotes, much studied by Japanese children from the ninth to the nineteenth century. She knows too some poems by Po Chü-i (the easiest of Chinese writers) and refers once to the Analects of Confucius.

In Japanese literature she knows the usual round of poems from the *Kokinshū* and *Gosenshū*. To speak, as European writers have done, of her vast acquaintance with Chinese literature, is an anachronism; for in her time only fragments of this literature had reached Japan. The great poets of the eighth century, for example, were entirely unknown. But the term 'learned' is in any case a relative one. A modern lady-in-waiting who had read a little Greek (or even only a little Gilbert Murray) would certainly pass as learned in her own circle; while at Girton no one would be impressed. And it is likely enough that the attainments by which Shōnagon dazzled the Palace would at the Fujiwara Academy have passed quite unnoticed.

It is, in fact, her extreme readiness of wit rather than her erudition that makes Shōnagon remarkable. I have not been able in my extracts to do her full justice in this respect, because in order to appreciate her allusions and repartees one must be in a position to grasp them immediately. Wit, more often than not, evaporates in the process of explanation.

But the brilliance of an allusion such as that to the Analects [1] may perhaps be vaguely surmised. That anyone possessed of such a gift, should enjoy using it seems natural enough. Almost every anecdote in her book centres round some clever repartee or happy quotation of her own. For this she has been reproached, and Murasaki has made her colleague's *shitari-gao* ('have done it!' look, i.e. air of self-satisfaction) proverbial. In life Shōnagon may indeed have been as insupportable as Murasaki evidently found her; but in the *Pillow-Book* her famous *shitari-gao* makes no disagreeable effect. We feel that Shōnagon displays her agile wits with the same delight as an athlete takes in running or leaping.

The Japanese excelled at portraiture. But the portraits that survive are those of statesmen and priests. The 'Yoritomo,' by Takanobu (the obstinate-looking man in black triangular garments squatting with a white tablet hugged to his breast[2]), and the Shōichi Kokushi (that old one-eyed priest spread out over a great arm-

[1] See above, p. 65.
[2] There is a good copy of this at the British Museum.

chair), by Chō Densu, are among the greatest
products of Japanese art. But I recollect no
portraits of women till a much later date.
Murasaki and Shōnagon we know only as
posterity imagined them—that is to say, as
conventional Court beauties of the Heian
period. One does not, however, in reading the
Pillow-Book, get the impression of a woman in
whose life her own appearance figured in any
very important way. Had she, on the other
hand, been downright ugly, it would have been
impossible to secure her a post as lady-in-
waiting. We may suppose then that her looks
were moderate. We certainly cannot accept the
argument of M. Revon: 'Si elle n'avait pas
été distinguée de sa personne elle n'aurait pas
raillé comme elle fait, les types vulgaires'—
reasoning which shows a fortunate unfamili-
arity with the conversation of plain women. But
we have no reason to doubt that Shōnagon had
many lovers. Stress is usually laid on her affairs
with Tadanobu, to which, however, she devotes
only some few, rather insipid pages. I imagine
that her real lovers were for the most part
people of her own rank; whereas Tadanobu,

rather circuitously (it was owing to his sister's marriage with the Empress's brother) soon became a *pezzo grosso*. But in the 'eighties of the tenth century he was well within Shōnagon's reach, and if they were ever lovers, it may have been before her arrival at Court.

Here is the longest passage which deals with their relationship:

Tadanobu, having heard and believed some absurd rumour about me, began saying the most violent things—for example, that I wasn't fit to be called a human being at all and he couldn't imagine how he had been so foolish as to treat me like one. I was told that he was saying horrible things about me even in the Imperial apartments. I felt uncomfortable about it, but I only said, laughing: 'If these reports are true, then that's what I'm like and there is nothing more to be done. But if they are not true, he will eventually find out that he has been deceived. Let us leave it at that. . . .' Henceforward, if he passed through the Black Door room and heard my voice from behind the

THE PILLOW-BOOK OF SEI SHŌNAGON

screens he would bury his face in his sleeve, as though the merest glimpse of me would disgust him. I did not attempt to explain matters, but got in the habit of always looking in some other direction.

Two months later matters had advanced some way towards a reconciliation, for Shōnagon writes:

He sent for me to come out to him, and (though I did not respond) we met later by accident. 'Darling,' he said, 'why have we given up being lovers? You know now that I have stopped believing those stories about you. I cannot conceive what is the obstacle. Are two people who have been friends for so many years really to drift apart in this way? As it is, my duties bring me constantly in and out of their Majesties' apartments. But if that were to stop, our friendship would simply vanish, with nothing to show for all that has taken place between us.' 'I have no objection to our coming together again,' I said. 'In fact, there is only one thing I should be sorry for. If we were seeing one another in the way you mean, I should certainly stop praising you [1]—as I constantly do at present—in her Majesty's hearing, with all the other gentlewomen sitting by. You won't, I am sure, misunderstand me. One is embarrassed under such circumstances, something inside one sticks and one remains tongue-tied.' He laughed. 'Am I then never to be praised except by people who know nothing about me?' he asked. 'You may be certain,' I said, 'that if we become good friends again I shall never praise you. I cannot bear people, men or women, who are prejudiced in favour of someone they are intimate with or get into a rage if the mildest criticism of someone they are fond of is made in their presence.' 'Oh, I can trust you not to do that!' he exclaimed.

I will end with a more general question. Women, it will have struck the reader, seem to play an inordinately large rôle in the literary life of the Heian period. How came they here to secure a position that their sex has nowhere else been able to achieve?

[1] The intimacy would, of course, be secret. Shōnagon's embarrassment would proceed solely from her own conscience.

As far as the production of literature went, women did not, in fact, enjoy so complete a monopoly as European accounts of the period would suggest. But convention obliged men to write in Chinese,[1] and not merely to use the Chinese language, but to compose essays and poems the whole attitude and content of which were derived from China. It may be objected that a potentially great writer would not have submitted to these restrictions—that he would have broken out into the vernacular, like Dante or Paracelsus. But this is to demand that a literary genius should also possess the many qualities essential to a successful reformer. The use of the native *kana* (the only form of character in which the Japanese language could be written with reasonable facility) was considered unmanly, and to use it would have made a writer as self-conscious as a London clubman would feel if he were to walk down Bond Street in skirts.

Women, anthropologists tell us, are often the repositories of a vanishing or discarded culture. And their conservatism becomes more

[1] Except in the case of *uta*, the small poems of thirty-one syllables.

marked where the mastering of a new script is involved; for women, though quick at acquiring spoken languages, have seldom shown much aptitude for the study of difficult scripts. To a minor degree, the same phenomenon was repeated in Japan a thousand years later. While the energy of male writers was largely absorbed in acquiring a foreign culture, and their output was still too completely derivative to be of much significance, there arose a woman [1] whose work, hitching straight on to the popular novelettes of the eighteenth century, has outlived the pseudo-European experimentations of her contemporaries. The fact that the men of the 'nineties in Japan were absorbed in imitating Turgenev does not, however, explain the occurrence of such a prodigy as Ichiyō (a working seamstress who in the years between nineteen and twenty-four produced twenty-five longish stories, forty volumes of diary, and six of critical essays); nor does the convention which obliged men to write in Chinese explain the appearance during the Heian period of such female geniuses as Ono no Komachi, Michi-

[1] Higuchi Ichiyō (1872–1896).

tsuna's mother, Izumi Shikibu, Sei Shōnagon and Murasaki—a state of affairs all the more remarkable seeing that from the fourteenth to the end of the nineteenth century not a single woman writer of any note made her appearance in Japan.

The following tables will facilitate comparison with the original:

TRANS. Page	ORIG. Sect.	TRANS. Page	ORIG. Sect.	TRANS. Page	ORIG. Sect.
24	301*	83	286, 291	118	24 A & B
25	160	84	89	119	295
32	32	88	82	121	270
34	3	90	48	123	132, 133
35	20	92	60	125	83, 109, 63
37	86	93	66, 230	127	183
56	124	94	87, 200	128	187, 113
58	75	95	257, 268	129	232
62	45	96	252	130	234, 271
68	72	101	263	131	235
73	156	103	103	132	285
77	194	112	287	133	284
78	94	113	31	135	297
80	46	114	30	139	6
82	46	116	21	155	116

ORIG. Sect.	TRANS. Page	ORIG. Sect.	TRANS. Page	ORIG. Sect.	TRANS. Page
3	34	83	125, 90	232	129
6	138	86	37	234	130
20	35	87	94	235	131
21	116	89	84	252, 257	96, 95
24	118	94	78	263	101
30	114	103	101	268	95
31	113	113	128	270	121
32	32	116	155	271	130
45	62	124	56	284, 285	133, 132
46	82	132, 133	123	286	83
48	90	156	73	287	112
60	92	183, 187	127	295	119
63	126	194	77	297	135
66	93	200	94	301	24
72, 82	74, 88				

*Preserved only in the so-called 'manuscript with the side-commentary.'

www.ingramcontent.com/pod-product-compliance
Lightning Source LLC
LaVergne TN
LVHW090013080525
810631LV00001B/17